51 PAPER CRAFT PROJECTS
for church, home and school

by Pat Karch

STANDARD PUBLISHING
Cincinnati, Ohio   2139

CONTENTS

Library of Congress Catalog Card No. 79-91249

ISBN: 0-87239-391-7

© 1979
The STANDARD PUBLISHING Company, Cincinnati, Ohio.
A division of STANDEX INTERNATIONAL Corporation
Printed in U.S.A.

HELPFUL HINTS

Tracing and Transferring a Pattern

1. To transfer a pattern from this book to the paper you are going to use, tape a piece of tracing paper or thin typing paper over the pattern. Trace with a soft-lead pencil. Turn tracing over onto paper to be used and retrace design on back of typing or tracing paper with a hard-lead pencil. By doing it this way your work will be neater, since no pencil marks will show on the right side.

2. If you are going to make several of the same item, tape the paper with the traced design on cardboard and cut out. This pattern can be used again and again by drawing around it.

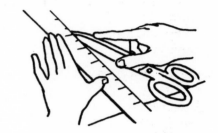

3. Another way to transfer patterns would be to blacken the back of a traced design with a soft-lead pencil, if you wish to transfer to a light-colored paper. Tape tracing, back side down, to paper you wish to use. Go over the lines of traced design on the right side with a hard-lead pencil. For dark-colored paper use chalk instead of a pencil on the back of tracing paper.

Scoring at Folds

To make cardboard or paper fold easily, run the blade of a pair of scissors or a dull knife lightly along fold line. Hold ruler against line as a guide to assure a straight fold.

Enlarging or Reducing a Pattern

Trace the pattern. Mark off this tracing with half-inch squares. Next, square off a piece of paper the size you wish the pattern to be. If you want to make the pattern larger, make the squares larger. If you want to make the pattern smaller, make the squares smaller. Number the squares the same way on both sheets. Place sheets next to each other and reproduce design on second sheet, one square at a time. Check numbers for correct position.

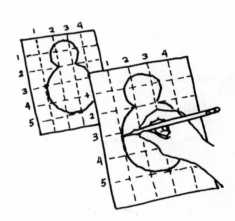

Curling Paper

To curl ends of paper, wrap the paper around a pencil and pull tight, or hold part of strip of paper between closed blade of scissors and thumb. Pull scissors gently but firmly along strip to end.

OR

Cutting and Gluing

Use a large pair of scissors or X-acto knife to cut cardboard and large areas. Use a small pointed pair of scissors to cut little things. Rubber cement is best for gluing large areas. White glue is fine for all other parts.

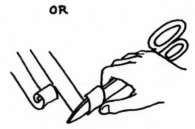

Bible Stories and Church

NOAH'S ARK

Materials needed: construction paper, glue, scissors

Place boat pattern on fold and cut out. Cut out deck. Cut ramp on one side of ark only so that you can glue deck ramp to it (Fig. 1).

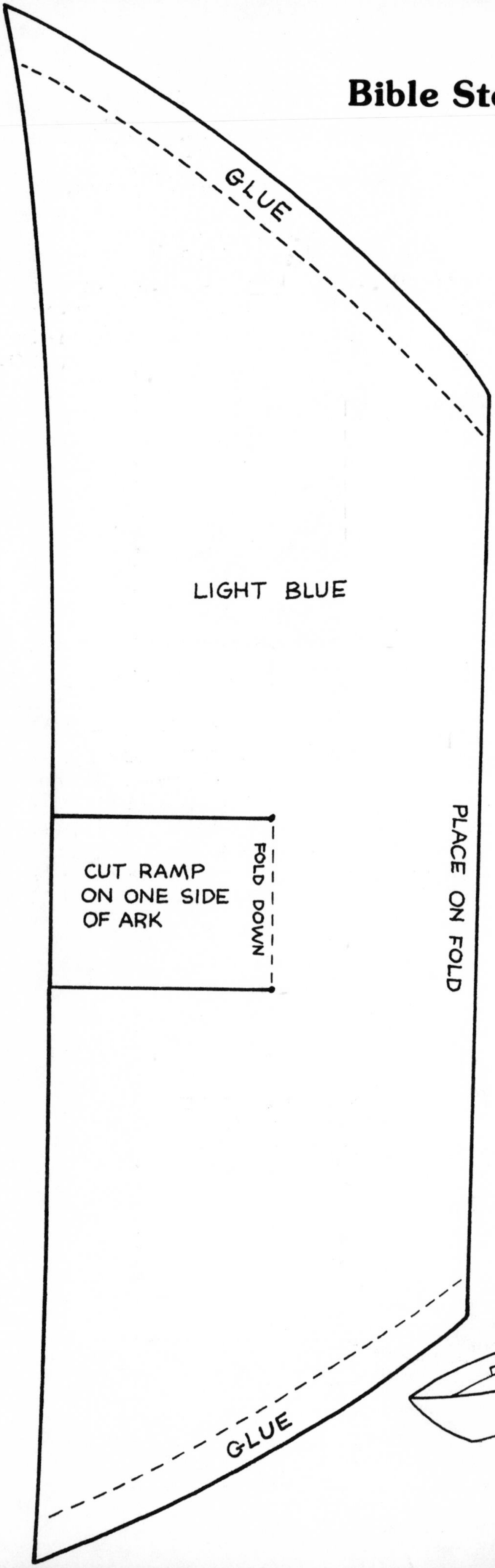

GLUE

LIGHT BLUE

CUT RAMP ON ONE SIDE OF ARK

FOLD DOWN

PLACE ON FOLD

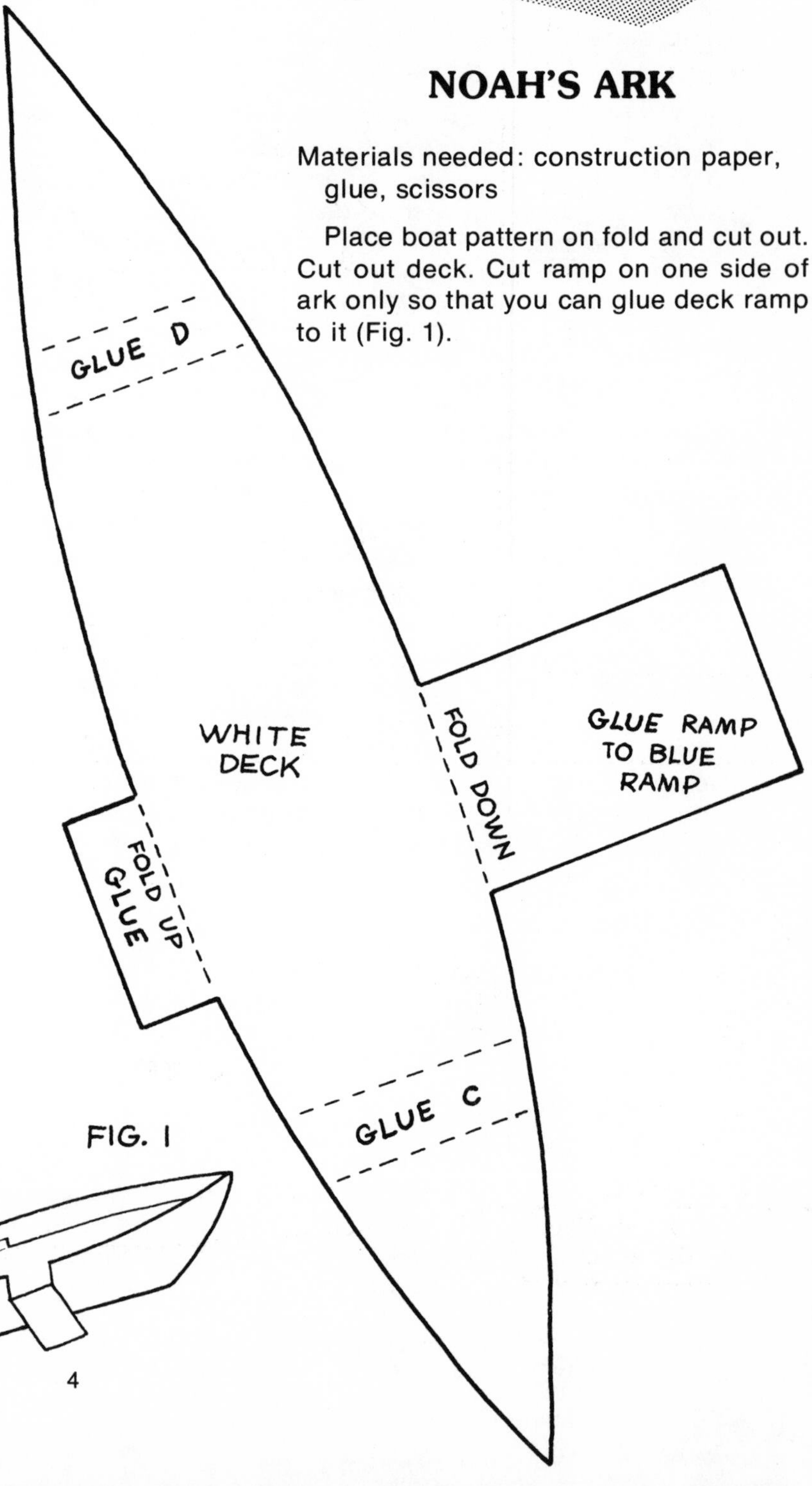

GLUE D

WHITE DECK

FOLD DOWN

GLUE RAMP TO BLUE RAMP

FOLD UP GLUE

GLUE C

FIG. I

GLUE

Cut out and fold cabin. Glue A to A and B to B. Glue onto deck at C and D. Place roof pattern on fold and cut out. Glue on roof (Fig. 2). Cut out dove and insert in slit in roof. Cut out window, and glue on. Ramp should form a stand to hold ark upright.

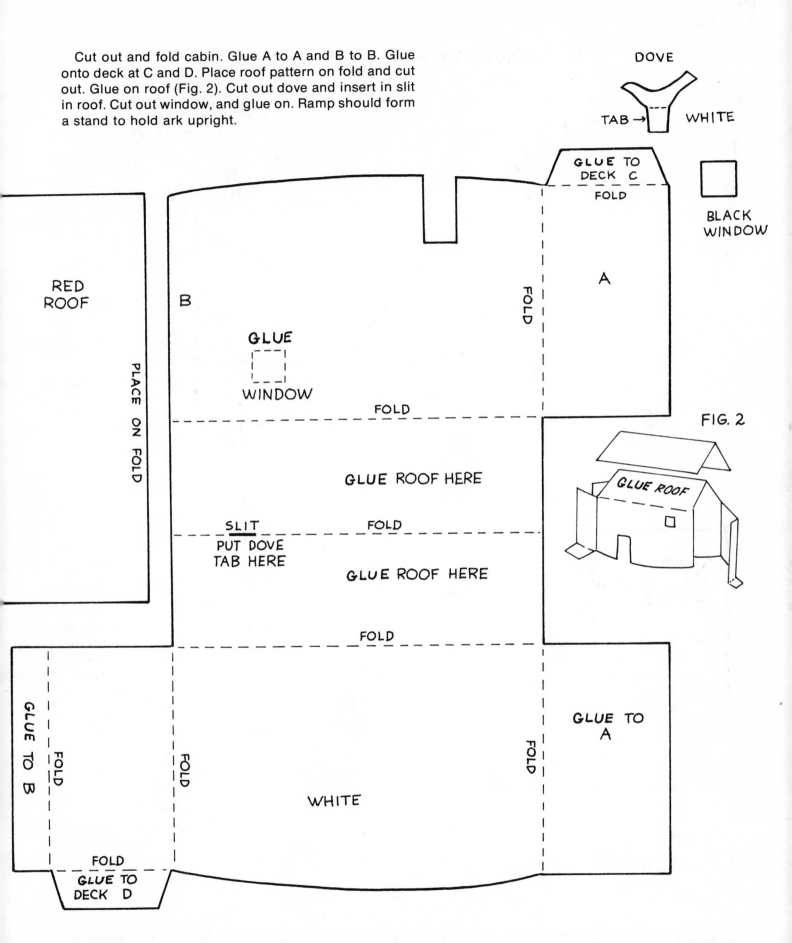

DOVE

TAB →   WHITE

GLUE TO DECK C

FOLD

BLACK WINDOW

A

RED ROOF

PLACE ON FOLD

B

GLUE

WINDOW

FOLD

GLUE ROOF HERE

FIG. 2

GLUE ROOF

SLIT

PUT DOVE TAB HERE

FOLD

GLUE ROOF HERE

FOLD

GLUE TO B

FOLD

FOLD

FOLD

GLUE TO A

FOLD

WHITE

FOLD

GLUE TO DECK D

HORN AND LYRE

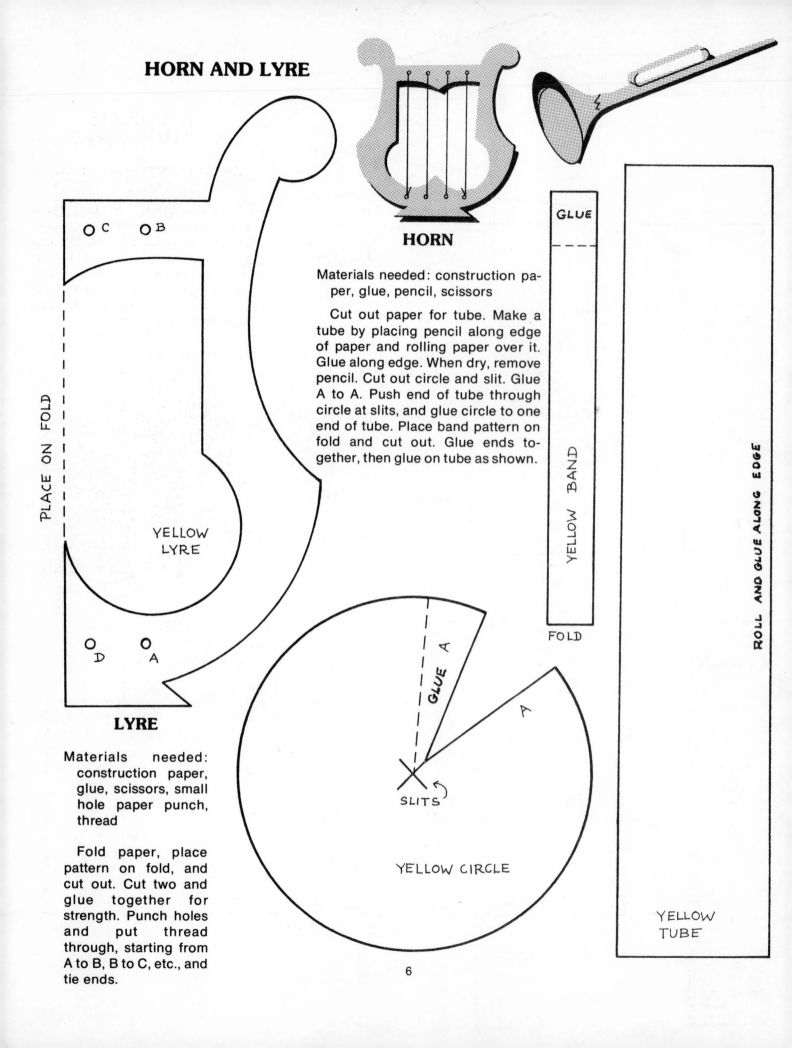

HORN

Materials needed: construction paper, glue, pencil, scissors

Cut out paper for tube. Make a tube by placing pencil along edge of paper and rolling paper over it. Glue along edge. When dry, remove pencil. Cut out circle and slit. Glue A to A. Push end of tube through circle at slits, and glue circle to one end of tube. Place band pattern on fold and cut out. Glue ends together, then glue on tube as shown.

O C   O B

PLACE ON FOLD

YELLOW LYRE

O D   O A

LYRE

Materials needed: construction paper, glue, scissors, small hole paper punch, thread

Fold paper, place pattern on fold, and cut out. Cut two and glue together for strength. Punch holes and put thread through, starting from A to B, B to C, etc., and tie ends.

GLUE

YELLOW BAND

FOLD

GLUE A

A

SLITS

YELLOW CIRCLE

ROLL AND GLUE ALONG EDGE

YELLOW TUBE

6

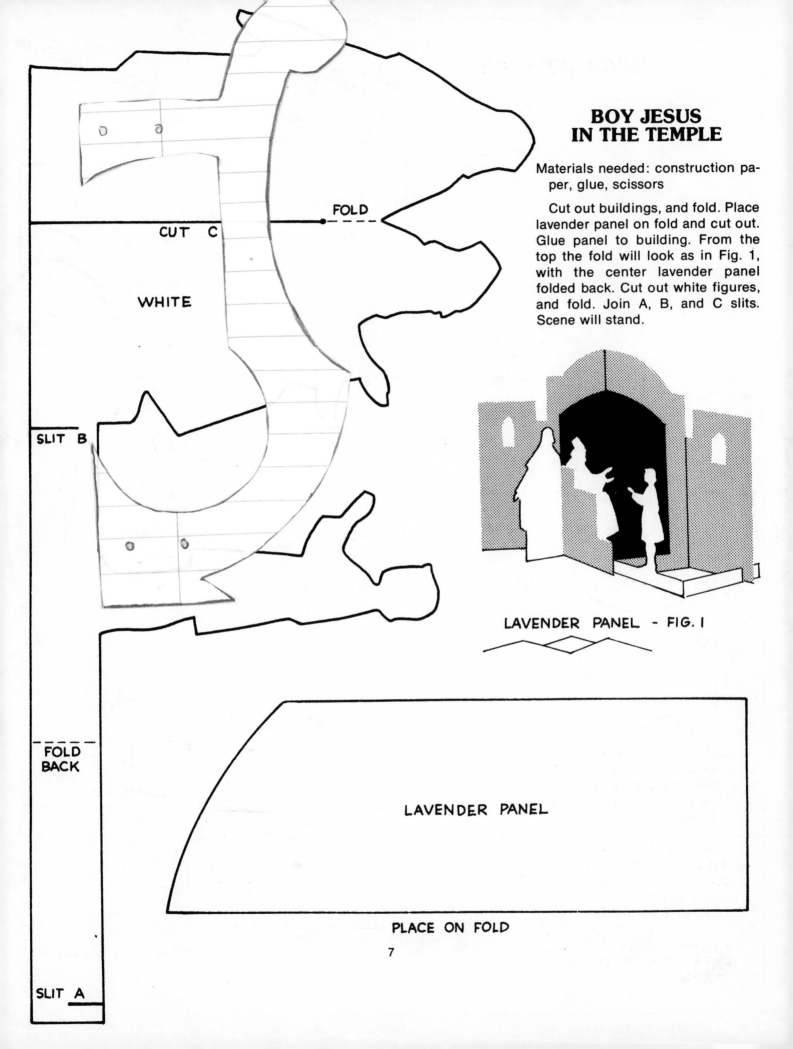

BOY JESUS
IN THE TEMPLE

Materials needed: construction paper, glue, scissors

Cut out buildings, and fold. Place lavender panel on fold and cut out. Glue panel to building. From the top the fold will look as in Fig. 1, with the center lavender panel folded back. Cut out white figures, and fold. Join A, B, and C slits. Scene will stand.

LAVENDER PANEL - FIG. 1

FOLD

CUT C

WHITE

SLIT B

FOLD
BACK

LAVENDER PANEL

PLACE ON FOLD

7

SLIT A

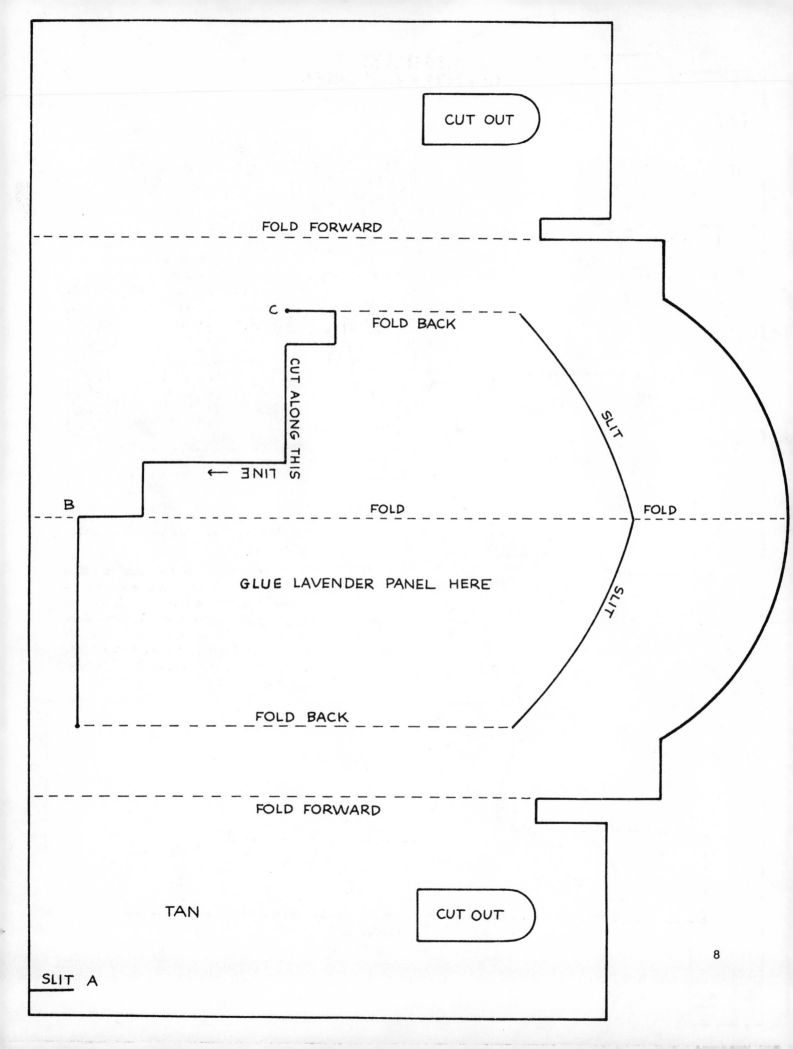

CUT OUT

FOLD FORWARD

C

FOLD BACK

CUT ALONG THIS LINE ←

SLIT

B

FOLD

FOLD

GLUE LAVENDER PANEL HERE

SLIT

FOLD BACK

FOLD FORWARD

TAN

CUT OUT

8

SLIT A

JESUS BLESSES
THE LITTLE CHILDREN

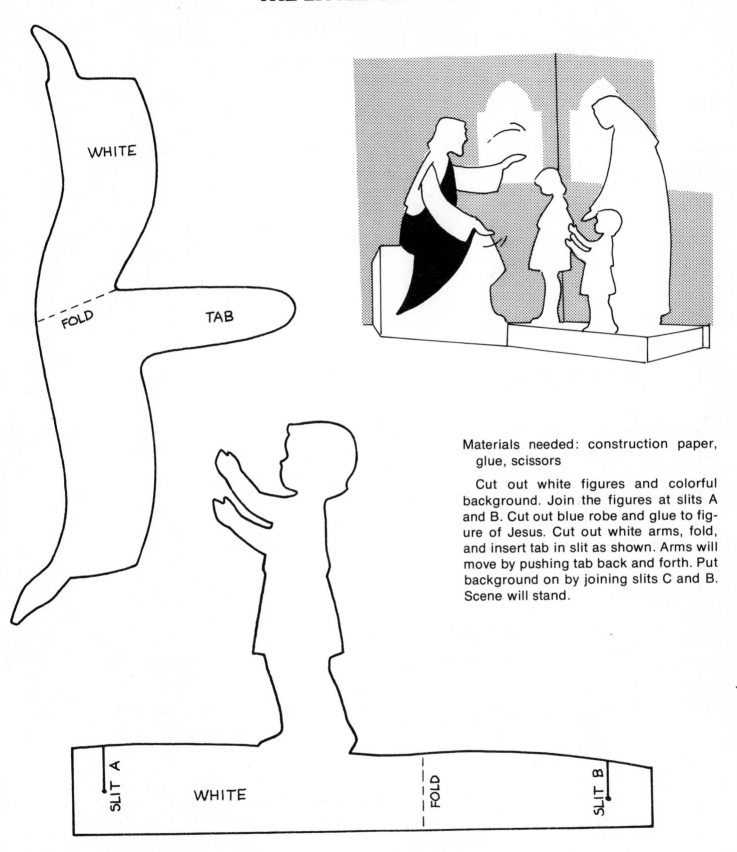

WHITE

FOLD

TAB

WHITE

SLIT A

FOLD

SLIT B

Materials needed: construction paper, glue, scissors

Cut out white figures and colorful background. Join the figures at slits A and B. Cut out blue robe and glue to figure of Jesus. Cut out white arms, fold, and insert tab in slit as shown. Arms will move by pushing tab back and forth. Put background on by joining slits C and B. Scene will stand.

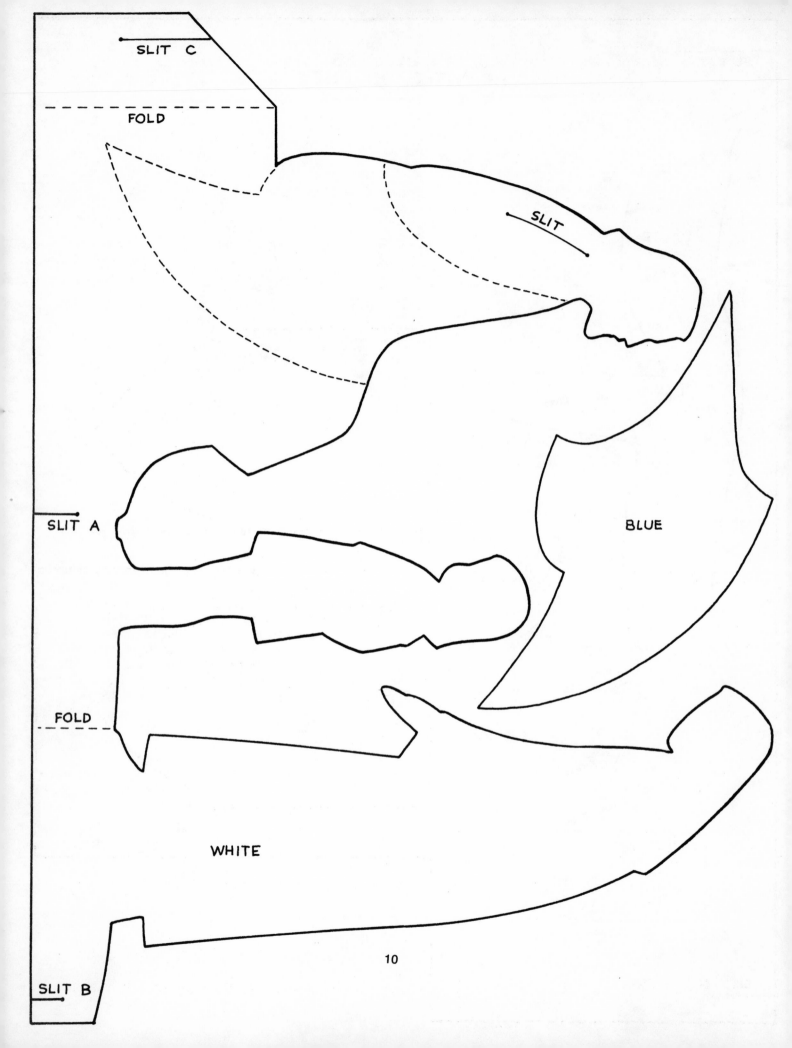

SLIT C

FOLD

SLIT

SLIT A

BLUE

FOLD

WHITE

10

SLIT B

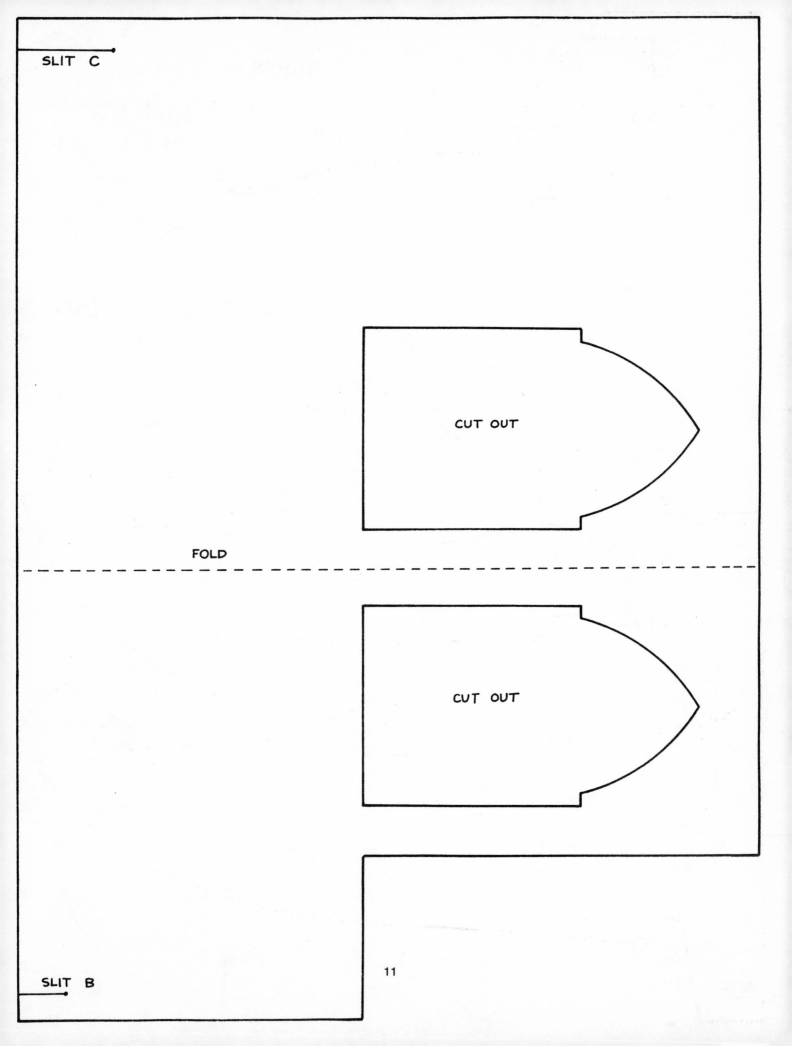

SLIT C

CUT OUT

FOLD

CUT OUT

11

SLIT B

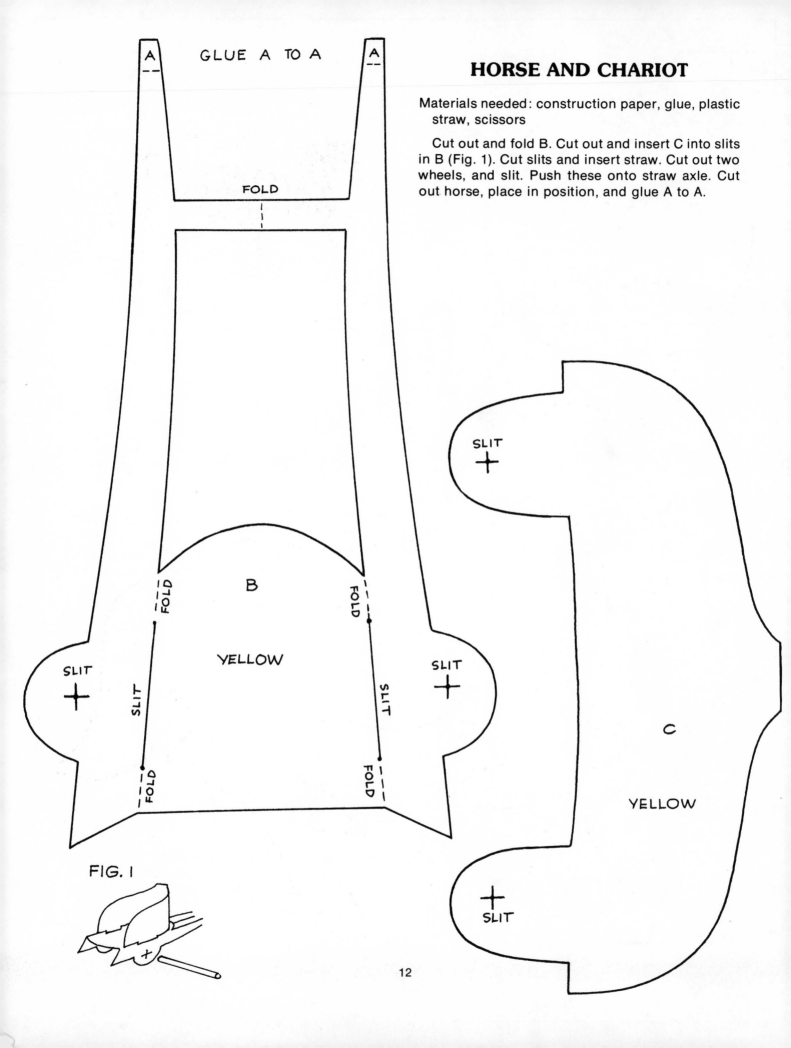

GLUE A TO A

A   A

FOLD

HORSE AND CHARIOT

Materials needed: construction paper, glue, plastic
  straw, scissors

    Cut out and fold B. Cut out and insert C into slits
in B (Fig. 1). Cut slits and insert straw. Cut out two
wheels, and slit. Push these onto straw axle. Cut
out horse, place in position, and glue A to A.

SLIT

FOLD   FOLD

B

SLIT   SLIT

YELLOW

SLIT   SLIT

FOLD   FOLD

C

YELLOW

FIG. 1

12

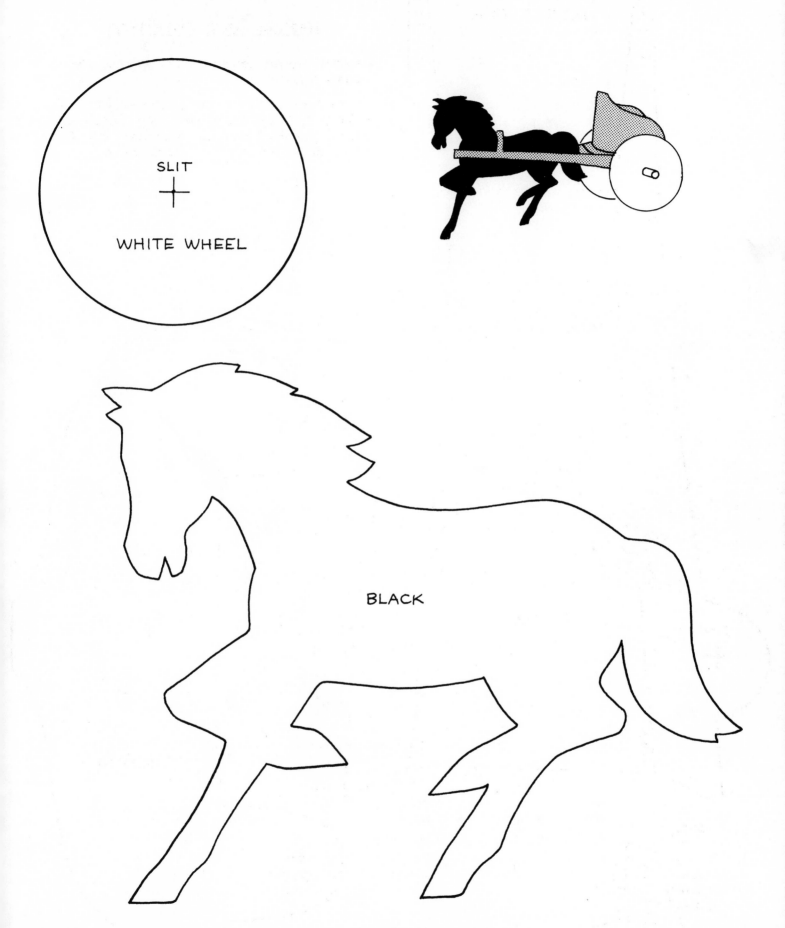

SLIT

+

WHITE WHEEL

BLACK

CHURCH BUILDING

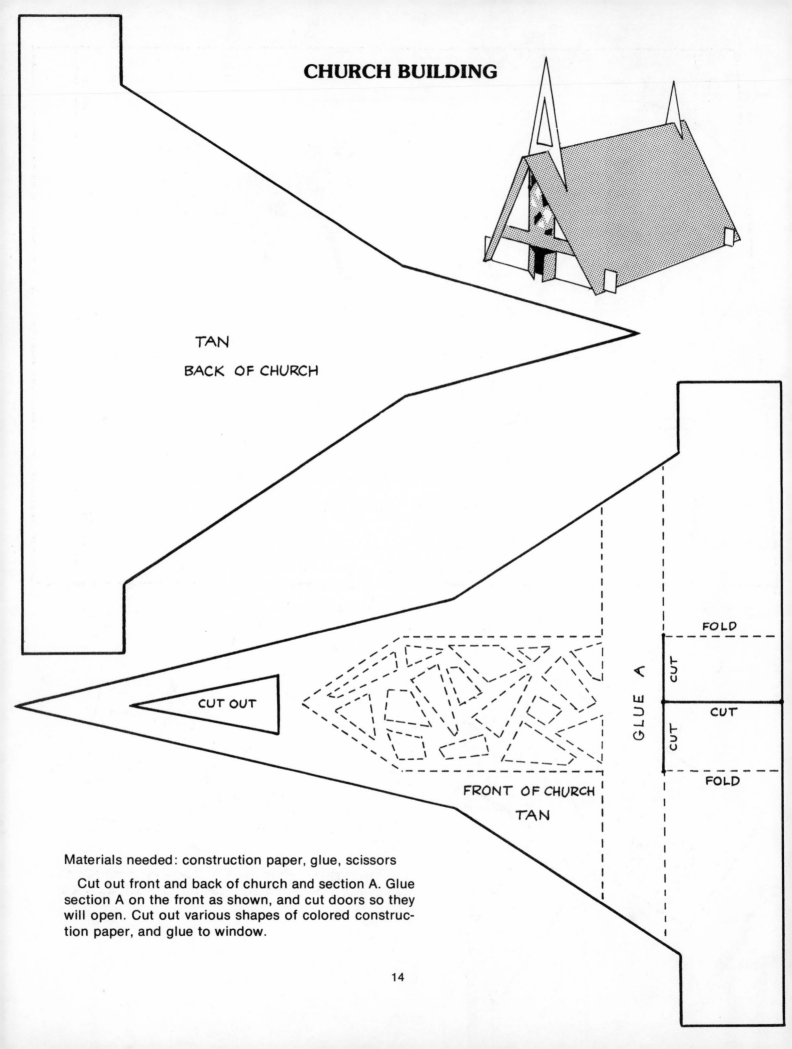

TAN

BACK OF CHURCH

CUT OUT

FOLD

GLUE A

CUT

CUT

CUT

FOLD

FRONT OF CHURCH

TAN

Materials needed: construction paper, glue, scissors

Cut out front and back of church and section A. Glue section A on the front as shown, and cut doors so they will open. Cut out various shapes of colored construction paper, and glue to window.

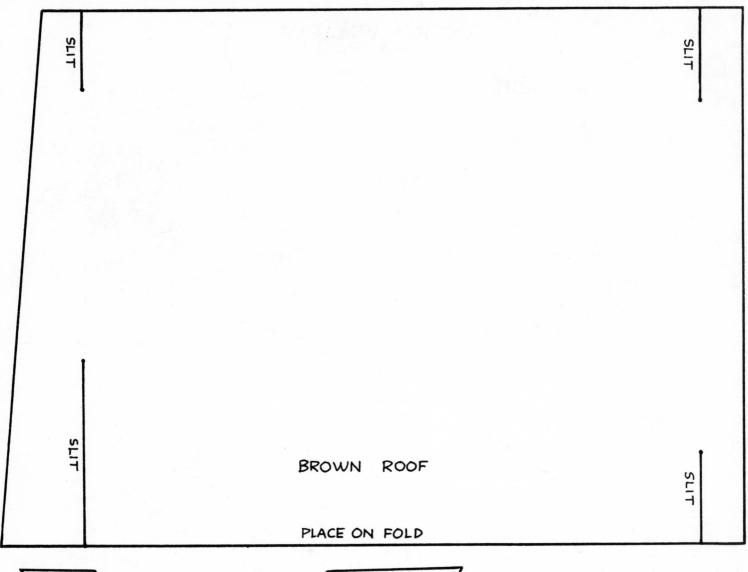

SLIT

SLIT

BROWN ROOF

SLIT

SLIT

PLACE ON FOLD

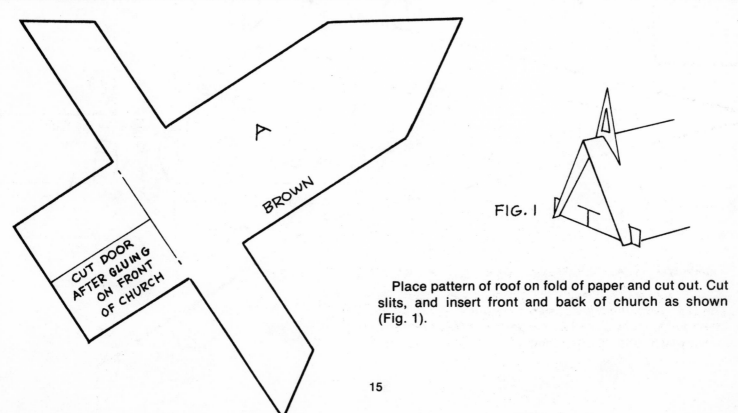

A

BROWN

CUT DOOR
AFTER GLUING
ON FRONT
OF CHURCH

FIG. 1

Place pattern of roof on fold of paper and cut out. Cut
slits, and insert front and back of church as shown
(Fig. 1).

15

God's Creatures

AQUARIUM

Materials needed: cellophane tape, construction paper, felt-tip pen, glue, 8-inch by 5-inch shallow box lid, scissors, thread

Glue a sheet of blue paper, 8 inches by 5 inches, in back of box lid. Cut out light blue or green ripples and glue to blue. Cut out pink coral and glue as shown. Cut out two each of goldfish. Glue together with thread in the middle. Draw eyes, gills, and scales on both sides of fish. Hang other end of thread to inside top of box lid with cellophane tape. The fish will swing about and turn like real fish.

Optional: Glue blue strips of construction paper to sides and bottom of inside aquarium.

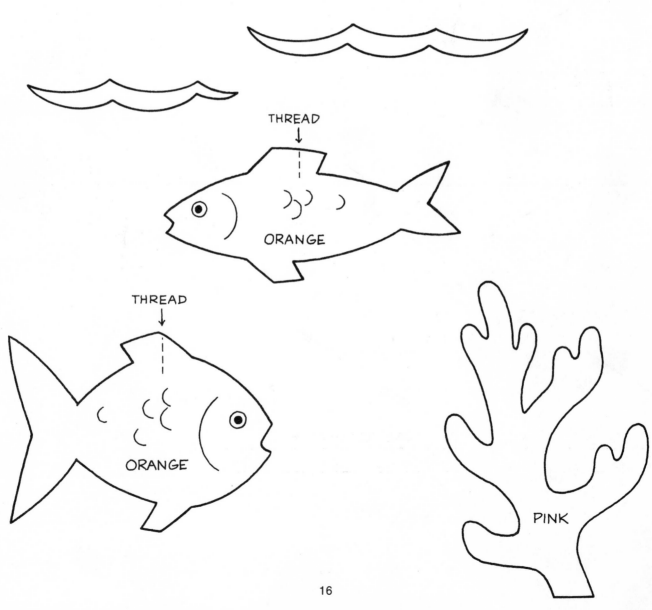

THREAD

ORANGE

THREAD

ORANGE

PINK

BIRD FEEDER

Materials needed: construction paper, felt-tip pen, glue, ⅜-inch wide ribbon, scissors, two large plastic straws

To make two birds, cut out four, and glue two together with four strips of ribbon between the tails. Do not glue wings. Draw eyes and cut slits. Run 4½-inch straws through slits.

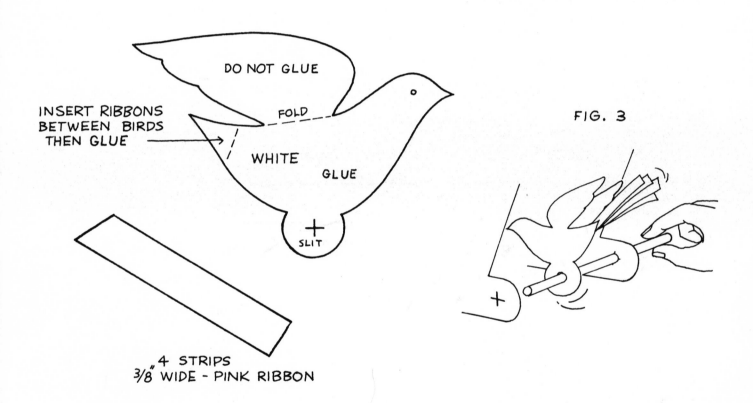

DO NOT GLUE

FOLD

INSERT RIBBONS BETWEEN BIRDS THEN GLUE →

WHITE

GLUE

+ SLIT

FIG. 3

4 STRIPS
⅜" WIDE - PINK RIBBON

TWO - 4½" PLASTIC STRAWS

17

Place roof pattern on fold and cut out. Cut out two sides and floor of feeder. Fold and glue roof, sides, and floor of feeder as shown (Fig. 1). Cut out hanger, glue C to C, then glue to center of roof (Fig. 2). Insert straws with birds through slits in feeder (Fig. 3). Turn straws for animation.

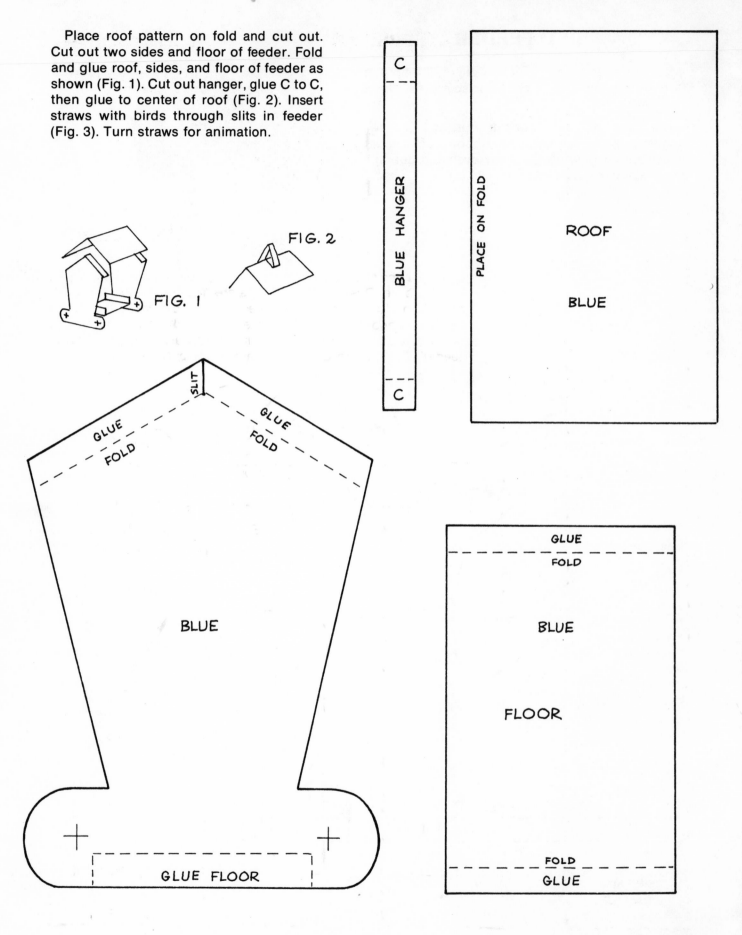

FIG. 2

FIG. 1

C

BLUE HANGER

C

PLACE ON FOLD

ROOF

BLUE

SLIT

GLUE

GLUE

FOLD

FOLD

BLUE

GLUE FLOOR

GLUE

FOLD

BLUE

FLOOR

FOLD

GLUE

CATERPILLAR

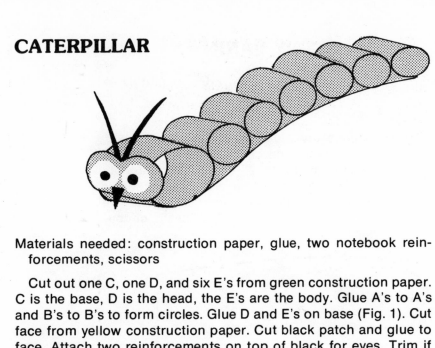

Materials needed: construction paper, glue, two notebook reinforcements, scissors

Cut out one C, one D, and six E's from green construction paper. C is the base, D is the head, the E's are the body. Glue A's to A's and B's to B's to form circles. Glue D and E's on base (Fig. 1). Cut face from yellow construction paper. Cut black patch and glue to face. Attach two reinforcements on top of black for eyes. Trim if needed. Cut out and glue red nose and two black feelers.

C

GREEN BASE

GLUE A

D

GREEN

A

GLUE B

E

GREEN

B

YELLOW

FIG. 1

RED

BLACK

BLACK

PUPPY BANK

Materials needed: black felt-tip pen, construction paper, glue, one 2⅛-inch by 3¾-inch frozen juice can with plastic lid, scissors

Cut out side panel and glue on can (Fig. 1). Place body pattern on fold of paper and cut out. Glue around can, overlapping white panel (Fig. 2). Cut out two ears and glue on each side. Cut out collar and glue as shown. Draw eyes, nose, and mouth with a black felt-tip pen. Cut top circle and top panel and glue on lid. Cut slit for coins with razor blade.

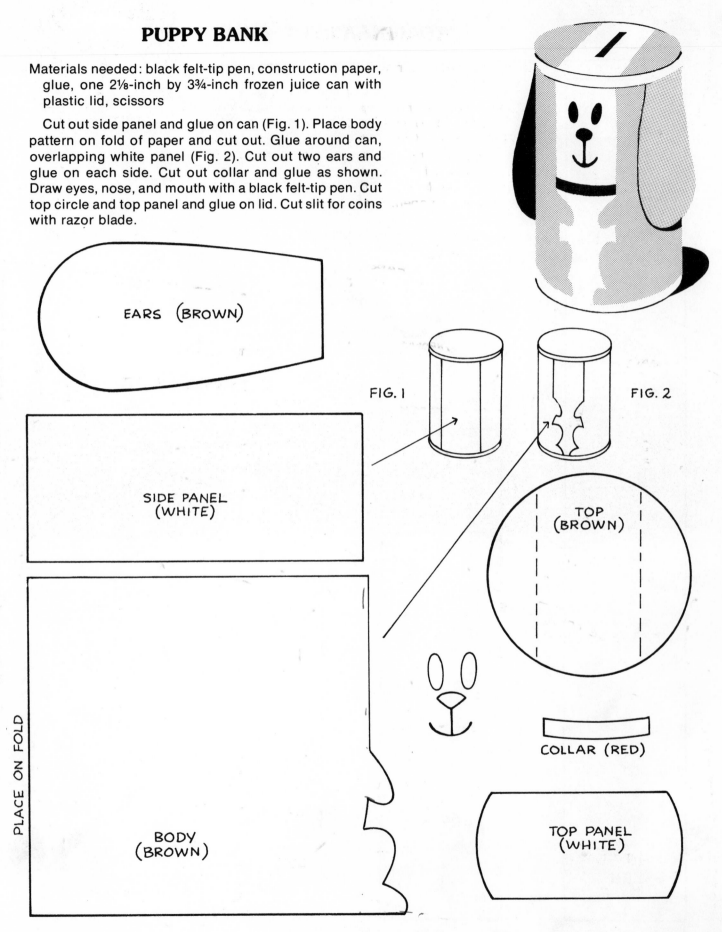

EARS (BROWN)

FIG. 1

FIG. 2

SIDE PANEL
(WHITE)

TOP
(BROWN)

COLLAR (RED)

PLACE ON FOLD

BODY
(BROWN)

TOP PANEL
(WHITE)

20

EYELIDS

ROARING LION

FOLD FORWARD

WHITE

RED
TONGUE

Materials needed: construction paper, felt-tip pen,
glue, scissors

Cut out lion and front legs. Glue legs in position.
Cut out lion's mane, nose, and two ears, and glue to
head. Cut slits in face. Cut out white eyelids and
mouth. Cut out red tongue and glue on white
mouth. Fold and insert this into slits from the back
of lion's head. Move from behind, making eyes
blink and mouth open. Draw eyes.

BLACK EARS

BROWN

BLACK

RED

GLUE
MANE

SLIT   SLIT

SLIT

GLUE
MANE

GLUE
MANE

SLIT

GLUE LEGS HERE
FIRST

FRONT LEGS

LIGHT ORANGE   FOLD   GLUE HERE ONLY

BROWN

LIGHT ORANGE

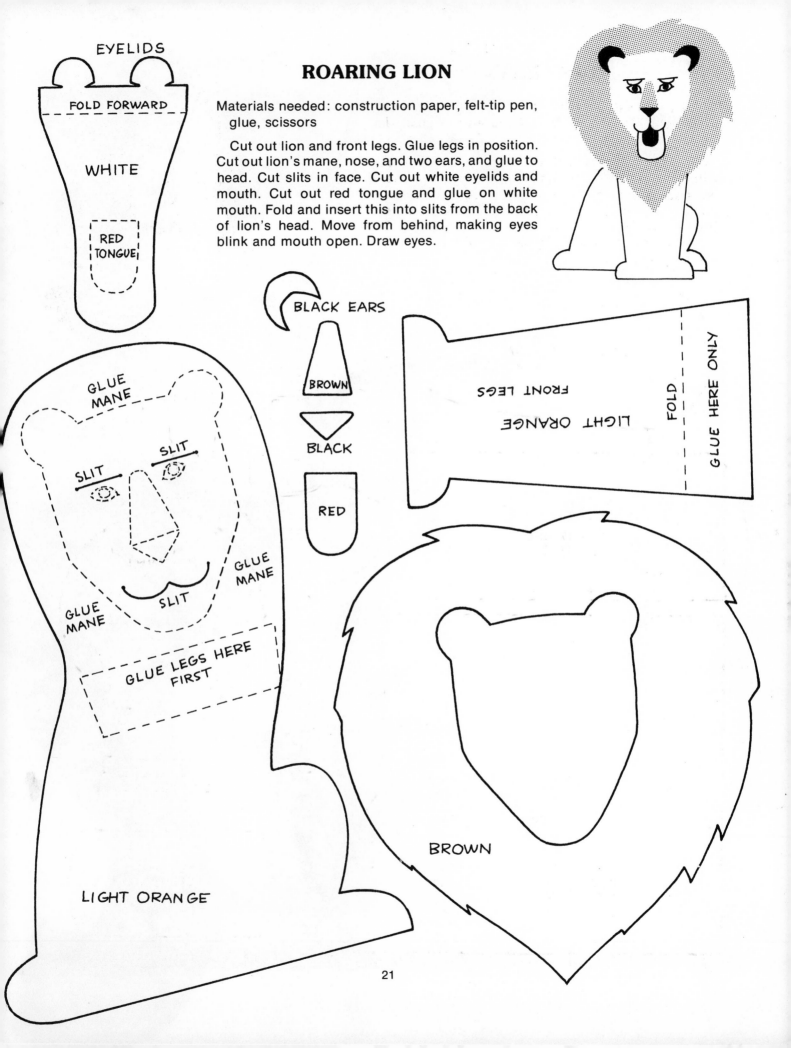

21

SQUIRREL WITH ACORN

Materials needed: construction paper, felt-
tip pen, glue, scissors

Place body pattern on fold of paper and
cut out. Cut out two tails and paws. Glue
tails together where indicated. With a felt-
tip pen, add lines to tail as shown.

Insert front paws through slits in bodies,
one on each side, then glue heads together.
Cut out and glue eyes, ears, and breasts.
Cut out and glue nut between tips of paws.
Move tail, and squirrel nibbles!

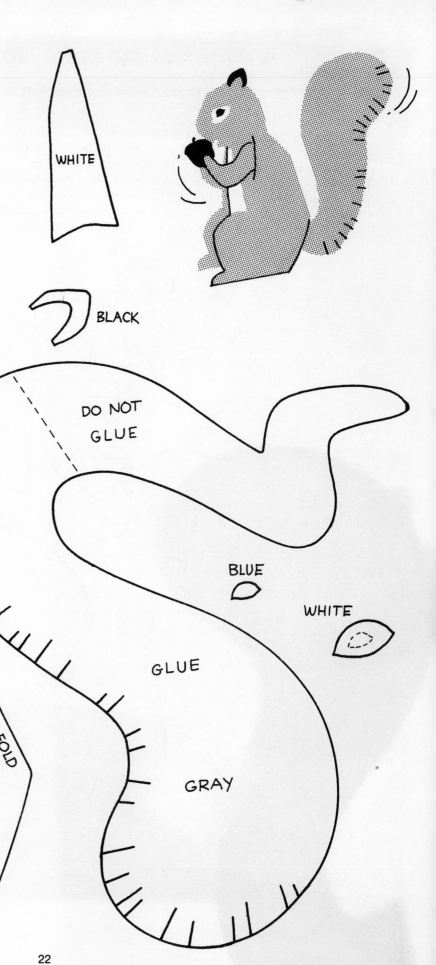

WHITE

BLACK

BROWN

DO NOT GLUE

BLUE

WHITE

GLUE

SLIT

PLACE ON FOLD

GRAY

GRAY

22

WALKING DUCK

Materials needed: construction paper, glue, paper fastener, scissors

Cut out two ducks. Cut out wheel and feet. Glue feet on both sides of wheel. Put wheel between ducks, and insert fastener at dots. Glue heads and tails of ducks together and cut slits. Cut out wings and insert through slits. Make duck walk by rolling forward on wheel. Finish by cutting out hat, trim, eyes, and bills. Glue these to both sides of duck.

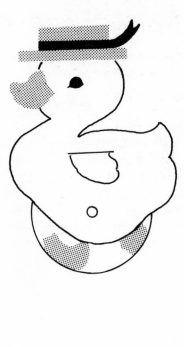

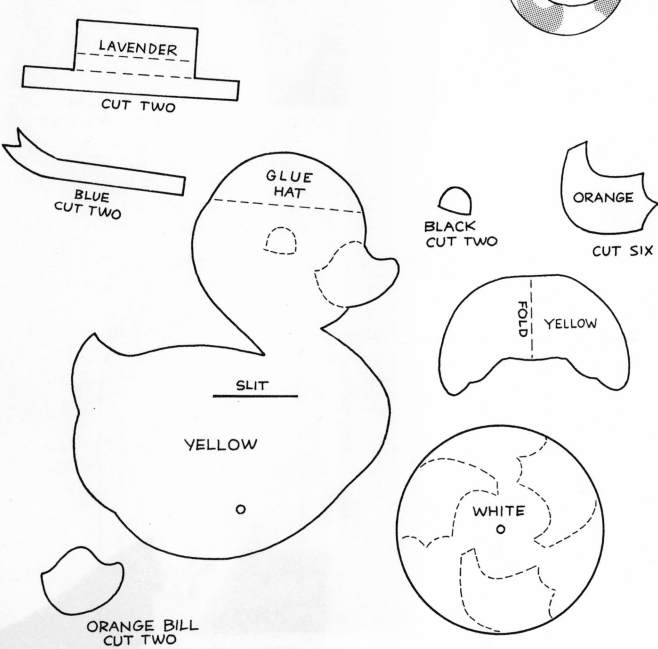

LAVENDER

CUT TWO

BLUE
CUT TWO

GLUE HAT

SLIT

YELLOW

ORANGE BILL
CUT TWO

BLACK
CUT TWO

ORANGE

CUT SIX

FOLD   YELLOW

WHITE

Spring

EASTER CARD

Materials needed: construction paper, glue, lavender tissue paper, scissors

Fold 9-inch by 12-inch white paper twice (Figs. 1 and 2). Cut out the church window on the first two pages. Glue a 3-inch by 5-inch sheet of lavender tissue paper between the first and second pages. Cut out and glue cross, lilies, and stem.

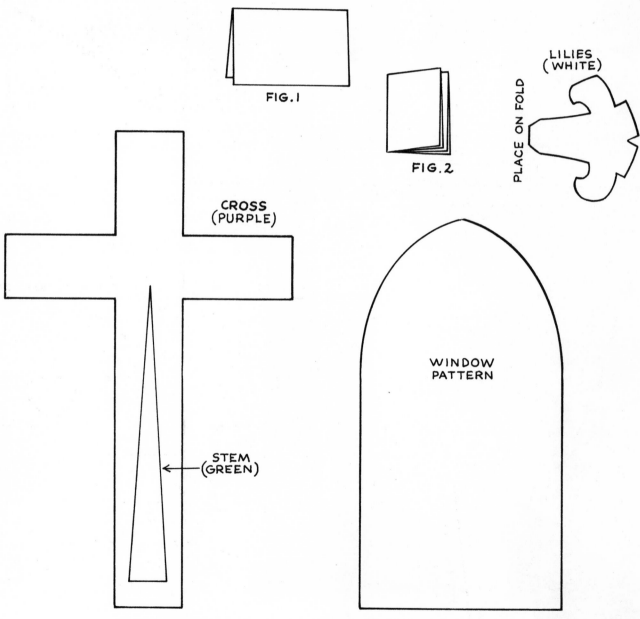

FIG.1

FIG.2

LILIES
(WHITE)

PLACE ON FOLD

CROSS
(PURPLE)

STEM
(GREEN)

WINDOW
PATTERN

MOTHER'S DAY CARD

Materials needed: construction paper, glue, scissors, felt-tip pen

Cut out A of light blue, B and C of white paper. Glue together as in Fig. 1. (Glue only the lower part of C so that a 2¼-inch by 1¾-inch card can be inserted as shown.) Cut out decorations, and glue as indicated. Draw lines with felt-tip pen.

To make envelopes see page 46.

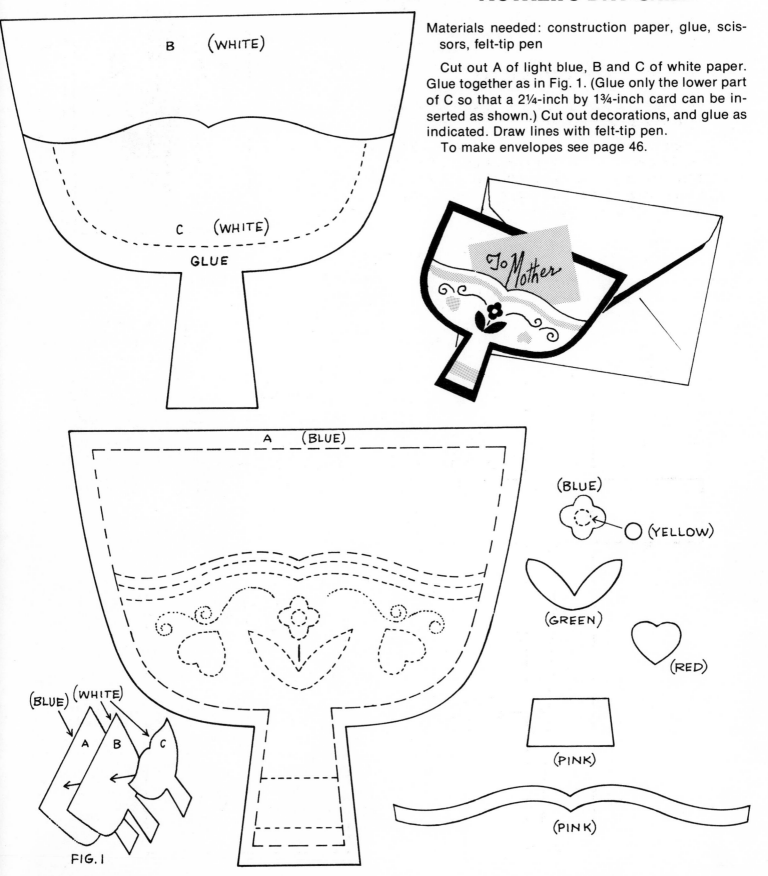

B (WHITE)

C (WHITE)

GLUE

A (BLUE)

(BLUE)

(YELLOW)

(GREEN)

(RED)

(PINK)

(PINK)

(BLUE) (WHITE)

A B C

FIG. 1

BASKET FOR MOTHER

Materials needed: construction paper, glue, scissors, tissue paper (pastel pink and blue variegated), ¾-inch satin paper ribbon (optional)

Fold a sheet of purple construction paper in half and place pattern on fold to cut out basket. Fold basket in half again along dotted line to cut out handle and make cuts for weaving ribbon in basket (Fig. 1). Cut out four 5¾-inch lengths of white ribbon or paper and weave as shown (Fig. 2). Glue ends to the basket to secure. Then clip excess even with basket. Fold basket and glue sides together.

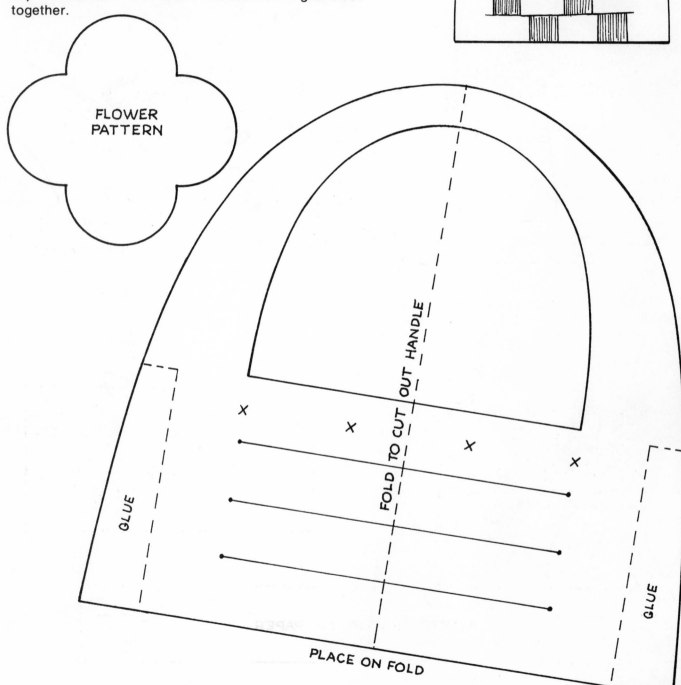

FLOWER PATTERN

FOLD TO CUT OUT HANDLE

GLUE

GLUE

PLACE ON FOLD

26

To make flowers, fold variegated tissue paper to several thicknesses (Fig. 3). Place pattern on top and cut all flowers at the same time. Pinch center of individual flower and twist (Fig. 4). Glue with dot of glue on X's indicated on both sides of basket. Cut out pastel card to place in basket with greeting written on it. You can vary the color combinations of baskets and flowers by using pastel spring colors.

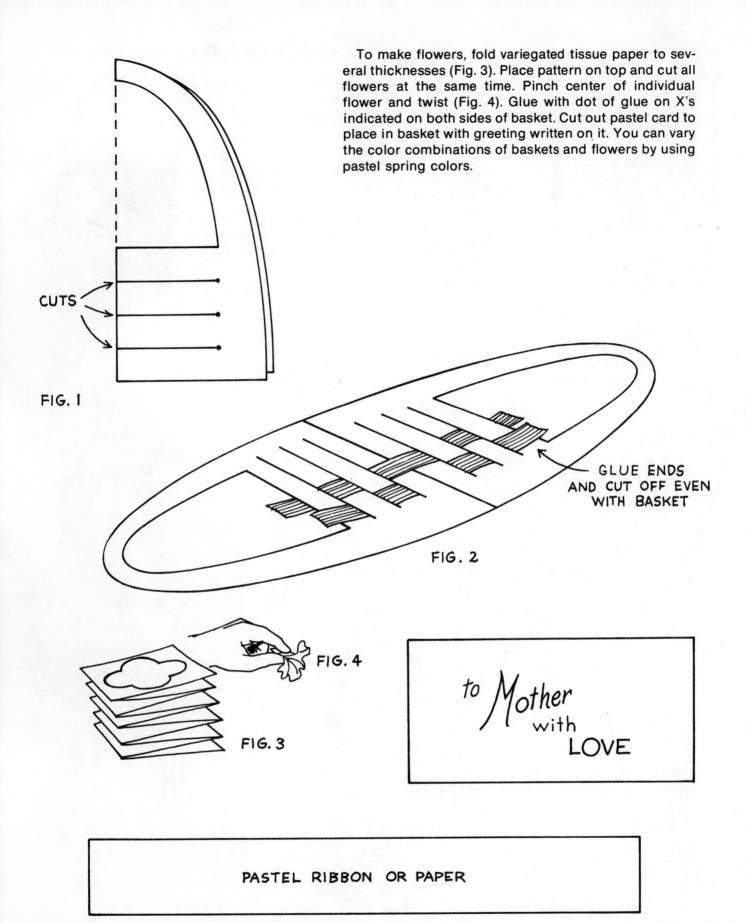

CUTS

FIG. 1

GLUE ENDS
AND CUT OFF EVEN
WITH BASKET

FIG. 2

FIG. 4

FIG. 3

to Mother
with
LOVE

PASTEL RIBBON OR PAPER

MOTHER'S DAY PICTURE

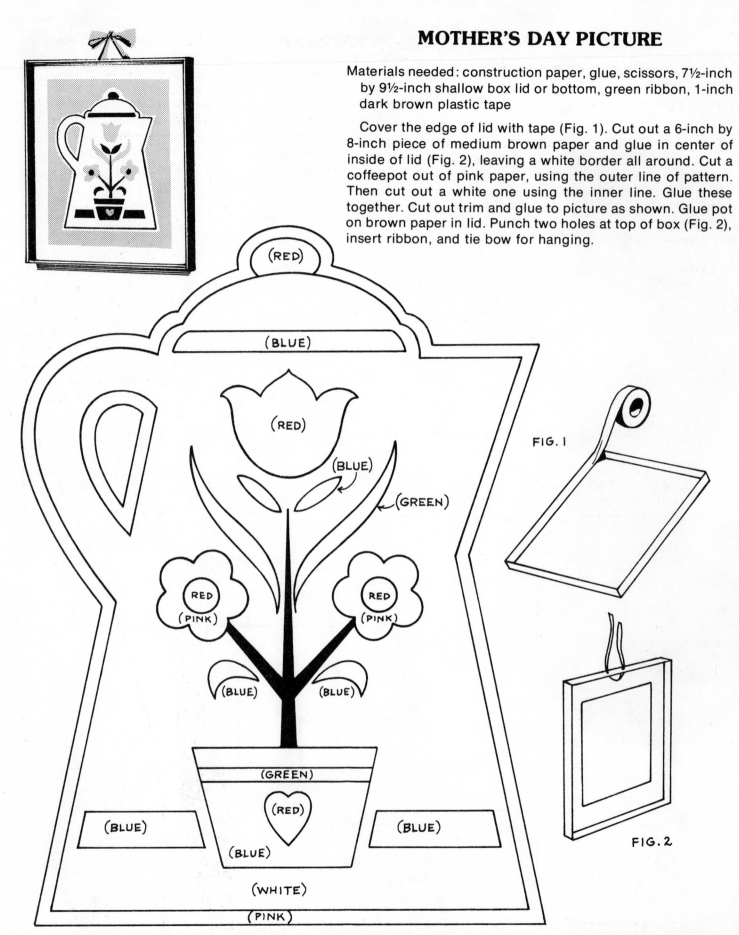

Materials needed: construction paper, glue, scissors, 7½-inch by 9½-inch shallow box lid or bottom, green ribbon, 1-inch dark brown plastic tape

Cover the edge of lid with tape (Fig. 1). Cut out a 6-inch by 8-inch piece of medium brown paper and glue in center of inside of lid (Fig. 2), leaving a white border all around. Cut a coffeepot out of pink paper, using the outer line of pattern. Then cut out a white one using the inner line. Glue these together. Cut out trim and glue to picture as shown. Glue pot on brown paper in lid. Punch two holes at top of box (Fig. 2), insert ribbon, and tie bow for hanging.

(RED)

(BLUE)

(RED)

(BLUE)

(GREEN)

RED (PINK)

RED (PINK)

(BLUE)

(BLUE)

(GREEN)

(RED)

(BLUE)

(BLUE)

(BLUE)

(WHITE)

(PINK)

FIG. 1

FIG. 2

FLOWERS TO MAKE

ALL-PURPOSE FLOWER

Materials needed: cardboard, glue, scissors, tissue paper

Cut out pattern A of cardboard. Place on top of stack of squares of tissue paper and cut many at one time (Fig. 1). Pinch and twist the center of each tissue and glue center to object to be decorated.

This all-purpose flower can be made of any color to complement your party color scheme. It is lightweight and glues easily to many patterns in this book.

TULIP

Materials needed: construction paper, florist clay, glue, gummed reinforcement, paper clip, paper straw, scissors

Cut out tulip in color desired. Glue A to A, B to B, etc. Secure with paper clip until glue is dry. Use a 5-inch length of straw. Make three slits in one end, and fold back ends to glue to bottom of tulip (Fig. 2 and 3). Slip a reinforcement on the straw and attach it to the tulip (Fig. 3) for added strength. Cut out two leaves and stick them in florist clay beside tulip. (Vary length of stems if you make more than one tulip.) A tulip can be placed in a nut cup or small paper cup, with a ribbon bow added.

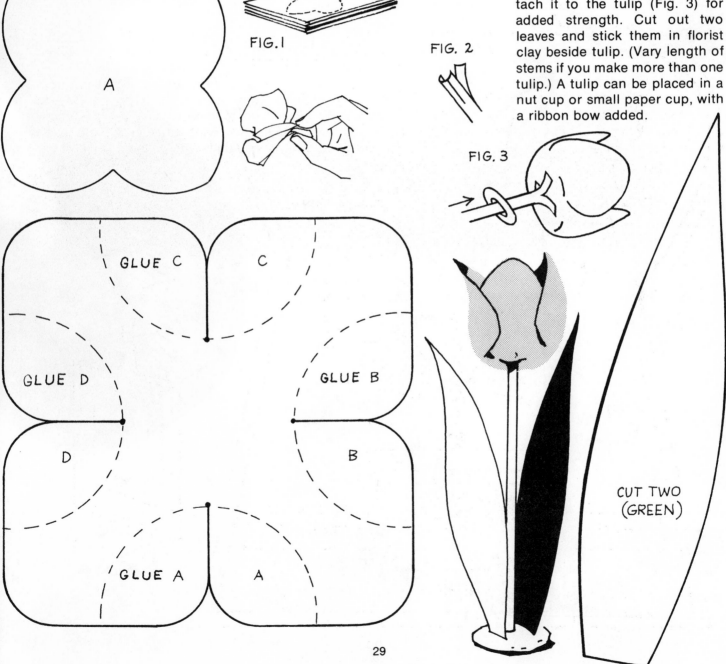

FIG. 1

A

GLUE C   C

GLUE D   GLUE B

D   B

GLUE A   A

FIG. 2

FIG. 3

CUT TWO (GREEN)

29

ROSE

Materials needed: crepe paper (red, white, pink, or yellow), construction paper, spool of florist wire, scissors

Cut strips from crepe paper as shown (Fig. 1), 2 inches in width and 8 inches in length. Fold the strips in half and cut scallops along one side (Fig. 2). Stretch the scalloped edges by pulling gently (Fig. 3). To form rose, roll and gather (at the same time) the straight cut edge (Fig. 4).

FIG. 1

Wind a 4-inch length of wire around the gathered end to hold. Curl back a few outer petals of rose (Fig. 5). Leave a length of wire to wrap around leaves cut from construction paper. Make garlands by wiring one rose to the next (Fig. 6), and pin to tablecloth. You will find many uses for the roses such as tying a rose with pink ribbon around rolled white napkins (Fig. 7).

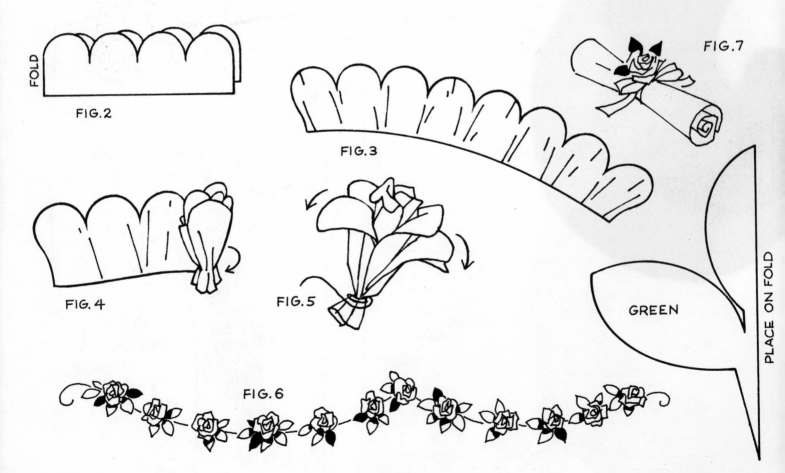

FOLD

FIG.2

FIG.3

FIG. 7

FIG. 4

FIG. 5

GREEN

PLACE ON FOLD

FIG. 6

Summer

WISE OWL PENCIL HOLDER AND CALENDAR

Materials needed: construction paper, glue, pencil, scissors, small calendar

Cut out two yellow owls with stand sections. Place owl pattern on fold of brown paper and cut out (Fig. 2). Cut out one side on dotted lines (Fig. 3) and glue this section to the yellow sections (Fig. 1). Fold yellow sections on dotted lines and glue together on part marked B to form stand.

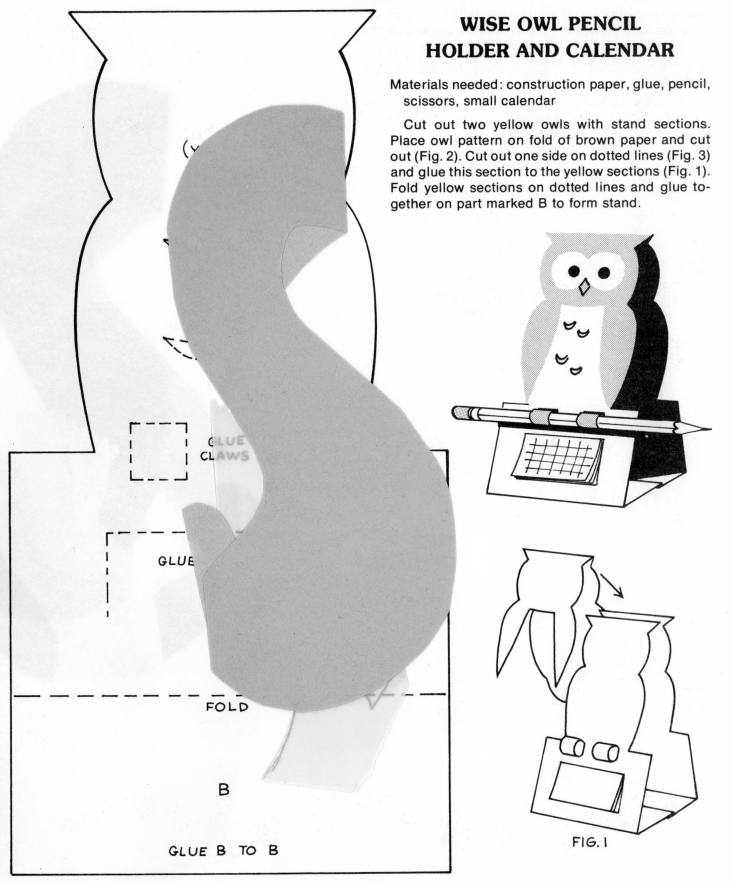

GLUE CLAWS

GLUE

FOLD

B

GLUE B TO B

FIG. 1

Cut out two claws, roll them over a pencil and glue A to A. Then glue to owl's body (Fig. 1). Cut out white eyes and glue on head. Cut out two black eyes and glue as shown. Cut out beak and glue in place. Cut out feathers and glue on breast. Glue small calendar to stand and insert pencil. This makes an excellent Father's Day gift to set on his desk.

FIG. 2   FIG. 3

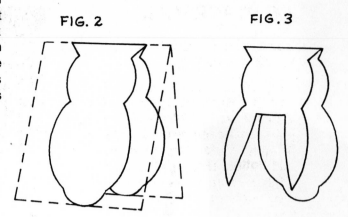

FIG. 4

EYES
(BLACK)

FEATHERS
(BROWN)

PLACE ON FOLD

(BROWN)

EYES
(WHITE)

PLACE ON FOLD

BEAK
(RED)

GLUE
EYES

CUT ALONG DOTTED LINE

A	CLAWS (ORANGE)	GLUE A

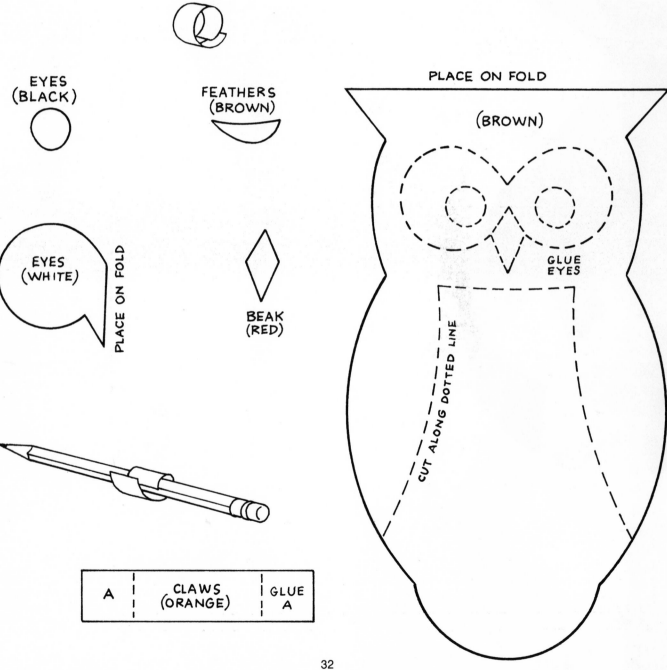

32

FLAG PLACE MAT

Materials needed: construction paper, glue, gold stars, scissors

Use a 9-inch by 12-inch sheet of red construction paper for the place mat. Cut out six 12-inch by 11/16-inch white stripes and glue on the red paper equally spaced, leaving an 11/16-inch red stripe at the top and bottom (Fig. 1). Cut out a rectangle of blue and attach stars to dots. Glue rectangle in upper left-hand corner of flag.

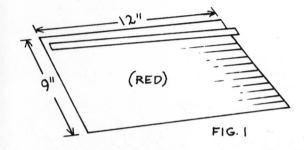

(RED)

12"

9"

FIG. 1

WHITE STRIPES

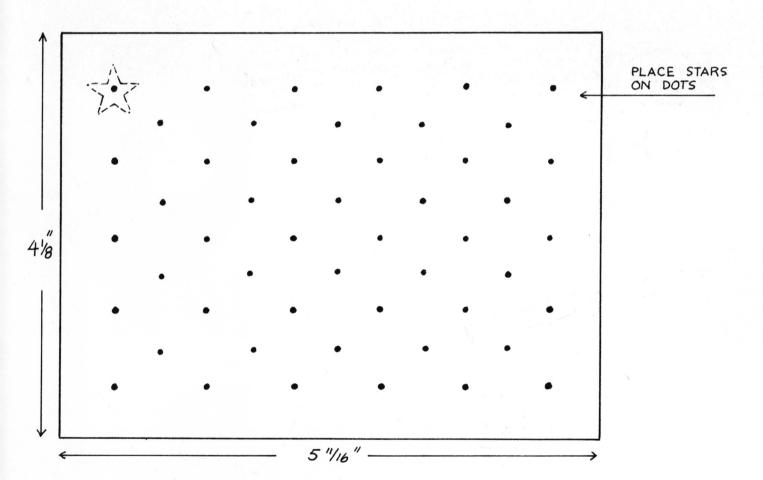

PLACE STARS ON DOTS

4 1/8"

5 11/16"

33

SPRINKLING CAN

Materials needed: construction paper, glue, scissors

Cut out can, and glue A to A. Cut out spout, fold, and glue B to B. Then glue spout to can. Cut out a purple handle, 7 inches by ½ inch, and glue as shown (Fig. 1). Cut out flower and leaves to trim can. Using the can pattern, cut out a pink trim to go around the bottom (Fig. 1).

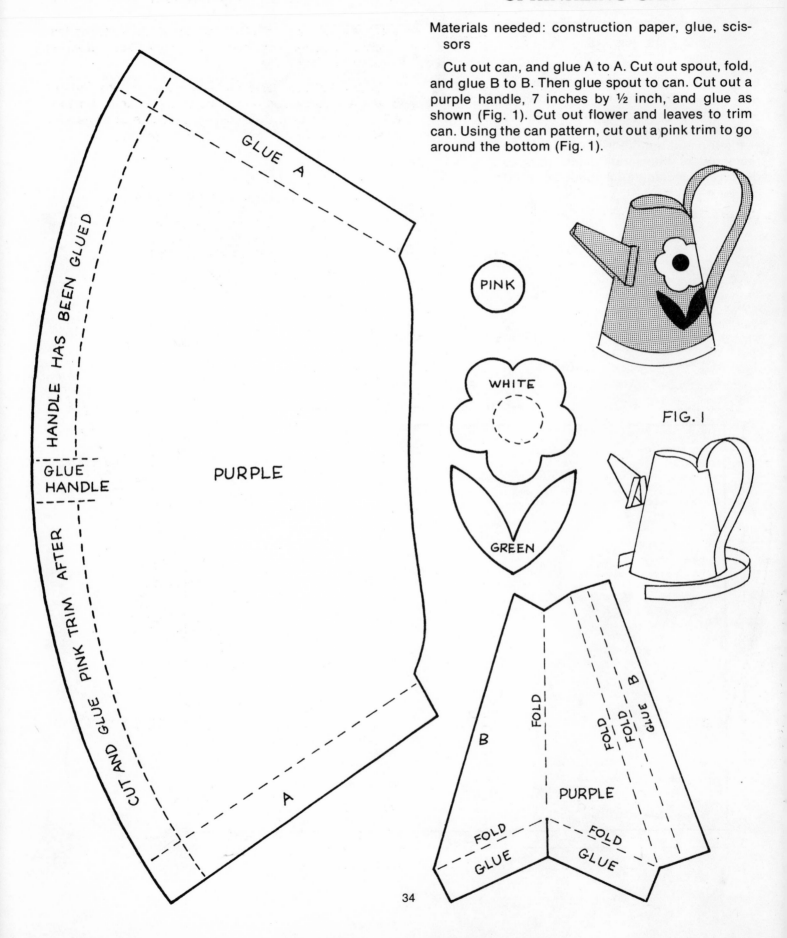

GLUE A

HANDLE HAS BEEN GLUED

GLUE HANDLE

CUT AND GLUE PINK TRIM AFTER

PURPLE

A

PINK

WHITE

GREEN

FIG. 1

B

FOLD

FOLD

FOLD

GLUE B

PURPLE

FOLD

FOLD

GLUE

GLUE

34

WHEELBARROW

Materials needed: construction paper, glue,
tener, scissors, two large paper straws, two
reinforcements

Cut out, fold, and glue wheelbarrow as shown
wheel and fasten between straws with paper
(Fig. 1). Put reinforcements around crossed s
push straws through to form handles (Fig. 2).

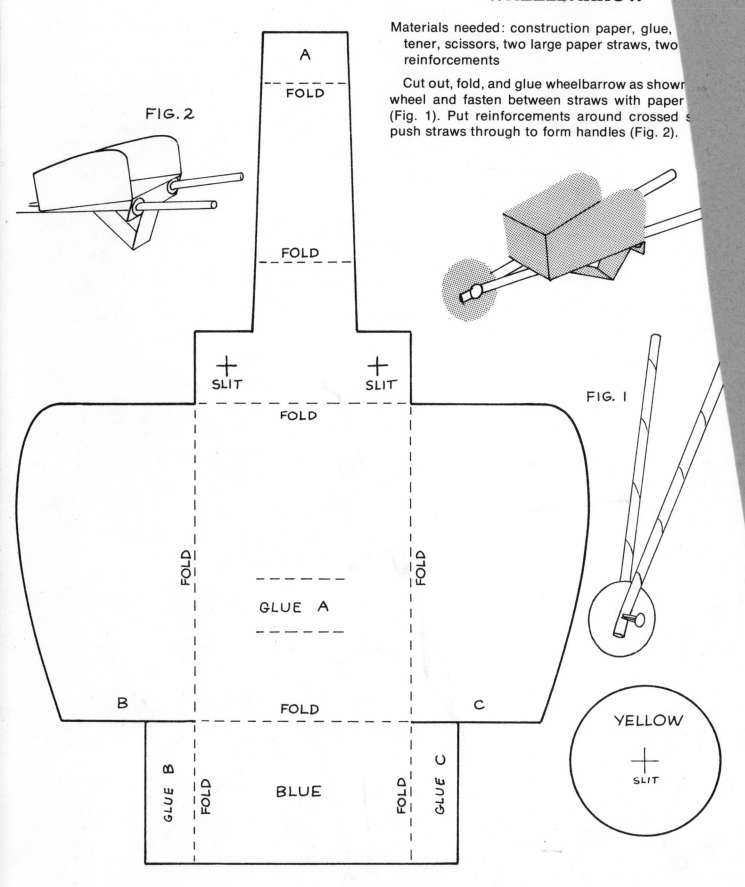

FIG. 2

FIG. 1

A

FOLD

FOLD

+ SLIT

+ SLIT

FOLD

FOLD

FOLD

GLUE A

B

FOLD

C

GLUE B

FOLD

BLUE

FOLD

GLUE C

YELLOW

+ SLIT

Fall   **CORNUCOPIA**

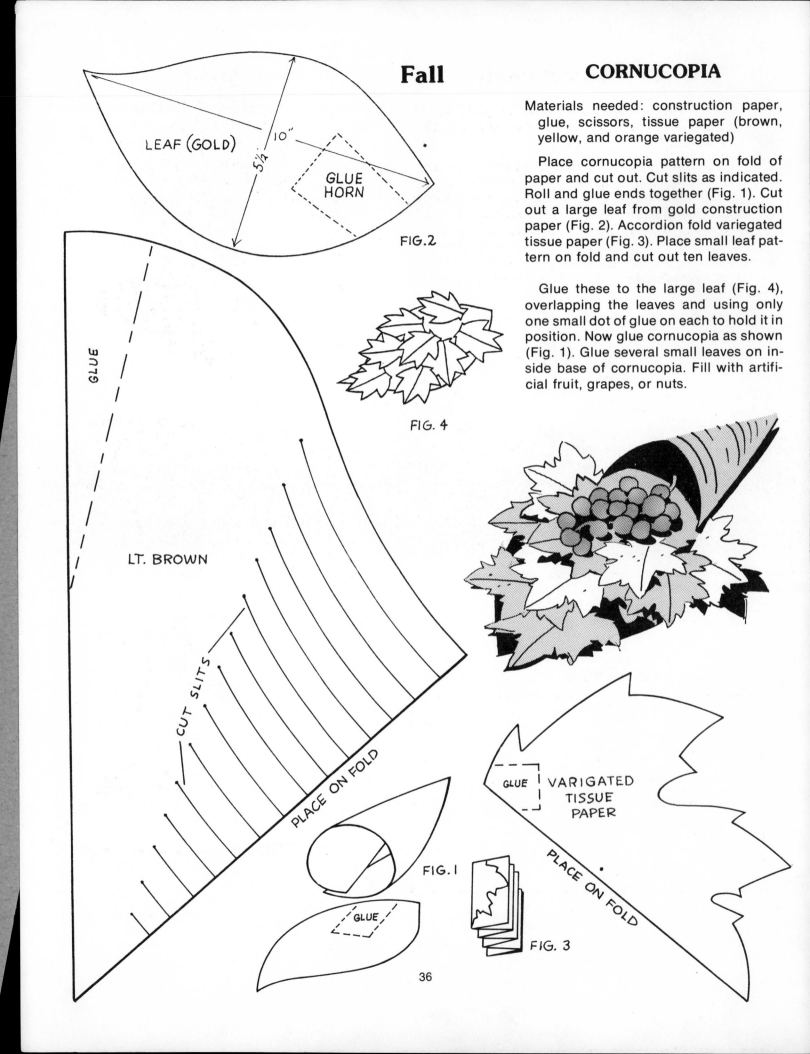

LEAF (GOLD)

10"

5½

GLUE HORN

FIG.2

GLUE

LT. BROWN

CUT SLITS

PLACE ON FOLD

FIG. 4

FIG.1

GLUE

GLUE | VARIGATED TISSUE PAPER

PLACE ON FOLD

FIG. 3

Materials needed: construction paper, glue, scissors, tissue paper (brown, yellow, and orange variegated)

Place cornucopia pattern on fold of paper and cut out. Cut slits as indicated. Roll and glue ends together (Fig. 1). Cut out a large leaf from gold construction paper (Fig. 2). Accordion fold variegated tissue paper (Fig. 3). Place small leaf pattern on fold and cut out ten leaves.

Glue these to the large leaf (Fig. 4), overlapping the leaves and using only one small dot of glue on each to hold it in position. Now glue cornucopia as shown (Fig. 1). Glue several small leaves on inside base of cornucopia. Fill with artificial fruit, grapes, or nuts.

TURKEY PLACE CARD

Materials needed: construction paper, glue, scissors, tissue paper (brown, yellow, and orange variegated), white cardboard

Place body and head patterns on fold of paper and cut out. Glue head to body. Cut a 20-inch by 3-inch strip of variegated tissue paper, and make small accordion folds as shown. Pinch one end and glue between body pieces (Fig. 1). Pull other end in fan shape and glue to outer sides of body. Fold a 3½-inch by 4-inch piece of white cardboard for the place card. Cut slits as shown and insert turkey.

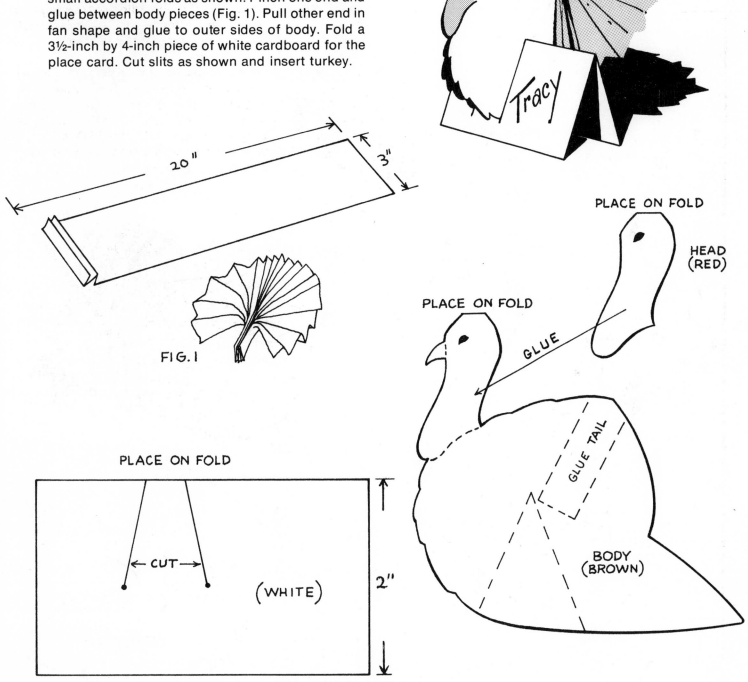

20"

3"

FIG. 1

PLACE ON FOLD

← CUT →

(WHITE)

2"

PLACE ON FOLD

HEAD
(RED)

PLACE ON FOLD

GLUE

GLUE TAIL

BODY
(BROWN)

TURKEY NUT CUP

Materials needed: chenille wire, construction paper, felt-tip pen, glue, large yellow paper baking cup, nut cup, scissors

Attach a 6-inch chenille wire to the nut cup (Fig. 1). Cut out two turkeys and wings. Glue two sides together over the chenille wire (Fig. 3). Cut slit for tail. Fold baking cup in half (Fig. 2) and insert in slit. Glue on wings. Cut out two waddles and glue on each side of head. Draw black eyes. Fill with nuts or candy corn. This is an excellent tray favor for a shut-in.

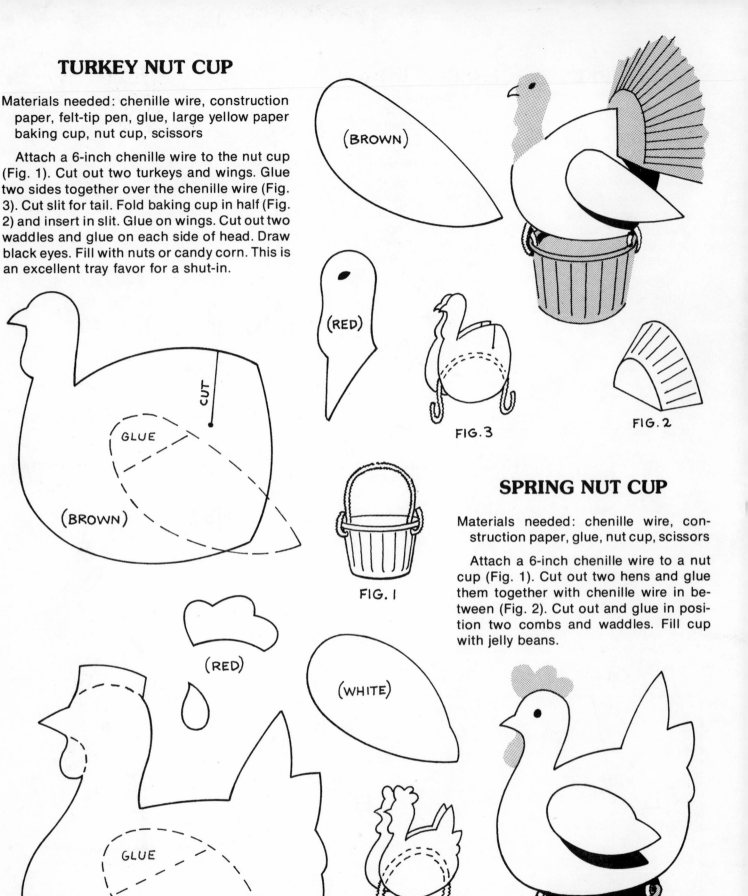

(BROWN)

(RED)

CUT

GLUE

(BROWN)

FIG. 3

FIG. 2

FIG. 1

SPRING NUT CUP

Materials needed: chenille wire, construction paper, glue, nut cup, scissors

Attach a 6-inch chenille wire to a nut cup (Fig. 1). Cut out two hens and glue them together with chenille wire in between (Fig. 2). Cut out and glue in position two combs and waddles. Fill cup with jelly beans.

(RED)

(WHITE)

GLUE

FIG. 2

(WHITE)

38

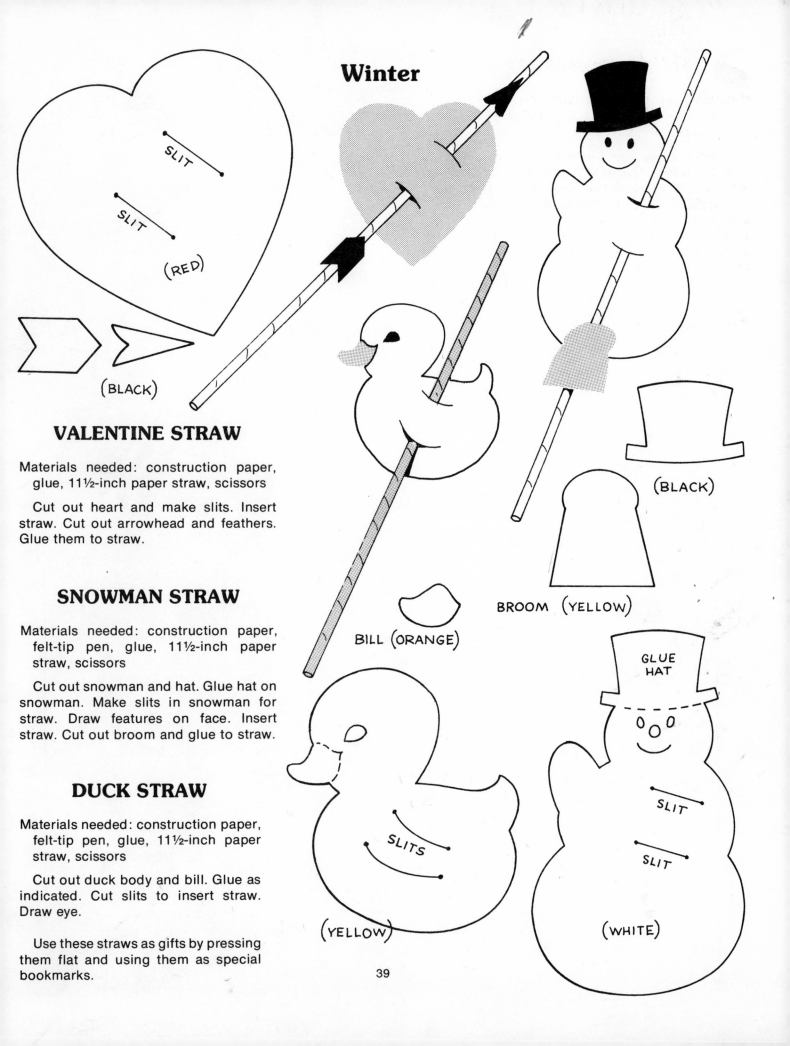

Winter

VALENTINE STRAW

Materials needed: construction paper, glue, 11½-inch paper straw, scissors

Cut out heart and make slits. Insert straw. Cut out arrowhead and feathers. Glue them to straw.

SNOWMAN STRAW

Materials needed: construction paper, felt-tip pen, glue, 11½-inch paper straw, scissors

Cut out snowman and hat. Glue hat on snowman. Make slits in snowman for straw. Draw features on face. Insert straw. Cut out broom and glue to straw.

DUCK STRAW

Materials needed: construction paper, felt-tip pen, glue, 11½-inch paper straw, scissors

Cut out duck body and bill. Glue as indicated. Cut slits to insert straw. Draw eye.

Use these straws as gifts by pressing them flat and using them as special bookmarks.

SLIT

SLIT

(RED)

(BLACK)

BILL (ORANGE)

(YELLOW)

SLITS

BROOM (YELLOW)

(BLACK)

GLUE HAT

SLIT

SLIT

(WHITE)

39

SNOWFLAKES

Materials needed: construction paper, foil paper, glue, paper fastener, scissors

Place pattern A on fold of white, gold, or silver paper, and cut out four. This will make the large snowflake. Join with paper fastener or glue in the center (at X). For B and C, fold paper twice (Fig. 1) and cut pattern as shown.

A

PLACE ON FOLD

C

PLACE ON FOLD

PLACE ON FOLD

B

PLACE ON FOLD

FIG. 1

PLACE ON FOLD

Christmas Cards

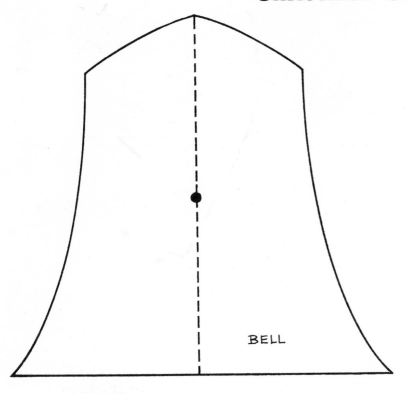

BELL

CUT TWO ~ ONE WHITE AND ONE DK. GREEN

BELL CARD

Materials needed: construction paper, glue, scissors

Fold 9-inch by 12-inch medium green paper twice (Fig. 1). Place white and dark green paper together and cut both bells from pattern. Cut a slit from the bottom to dot on white bell. Cut slit from top down to dot on green bell (Fig. 2). Slide them together (Fig. 3). Lay them flat and glue to folder. Cut out trim, and glue to flattened bells (Fig. 4). Cut out clapper and ball, and glue in position. Bell opens when you stand card.

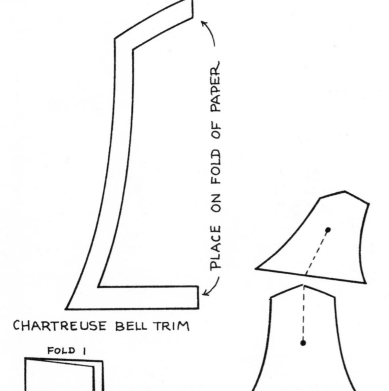

PLACE ON FOLD OF PAPER

CHARTREUSE BELL TRIM

FOLD 1

FOLD 2

FIG. 1

FIG. 2

FIG. 3

RED CLAPPER

RED BALL

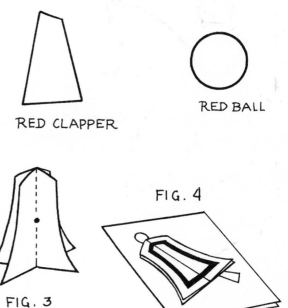

FIG. 4

BETHLEHEM CARD

Materials needed: construction paper, glue, scissors

Fold 9-inch by 12-inch dark blue paper twice (Fig. 1). Fold purple paper in half, place scene pattern on fold, and cut out. Cut out hills, and glue on bottom of folder. Glue scene onto hills. Cut out strips, and glue on to form star.

FIG. 1

FOLD 1

FOLD 2

WHITE STAR STRIPS

PURPLE SCENE

PLACE ON FOLD

LAVENDER HILLS

KINGS AND SHEPHERD CARD

Materials needed: construction paper, glue, scissors

Fold 9-inch by 12-inch purple paper twice (Fig. 1). Cut staff, and glue to folder. Cut three crowns, and glue to folder as shown. Decorate with trims and diamonds.

FIG. 1

FOLD 1

FOLD 2

BROWN STAFF

YELLOW CROWN

RED DIAMOND

ORANGE TRIM

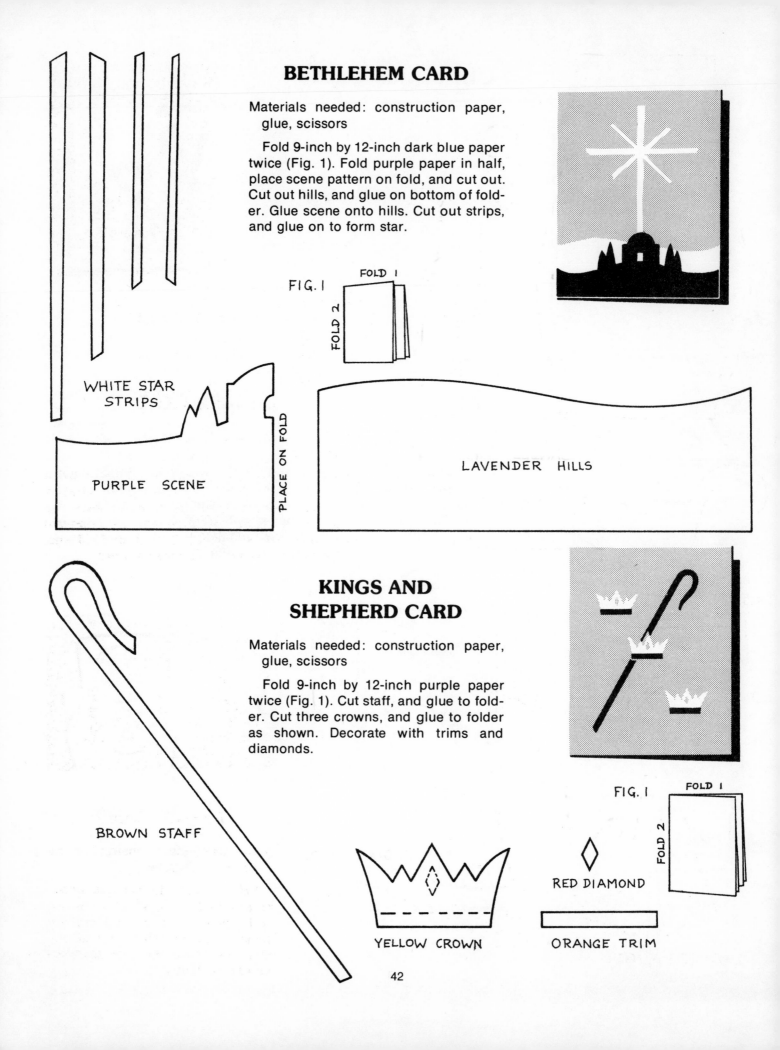

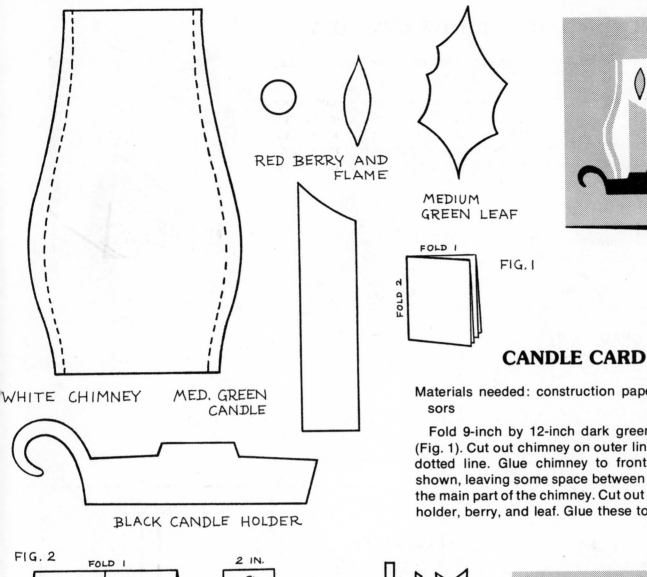

RED BERRY AND
FLAME

MEDIUM
GREEN LEAF

WHITE CHIMNEY   MED. GREEN
CANDLE

BLACK CANDLE HOLDER

FOLD 1

FOLD 2

FIG. 1

CANDLE CARD

Materials needed: construction paper, glue, scissors

Fold 9-inch by 12-inch dark green paper twice (Fig. 1). Cut out chimney on outer line, then cut on dotted line. Glue chimney to front of folder as shown, leaving some space between the strips and the main part of the chimney. Cut out candle, flame, holder, berry, and leaf. Glue these to card.

FIG. 2

FOLD 1

FOLD 2

2 IN.

3 IN.

FIG. 3

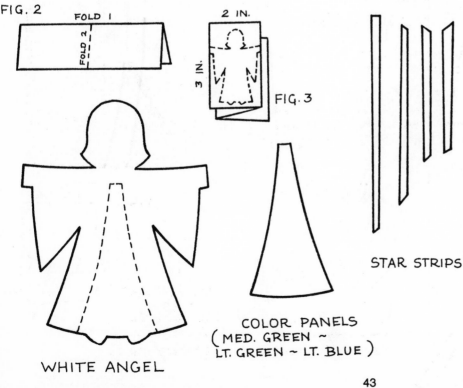

WHITE ANGEL

COLOR PANELS
(MED. GREEN ~
LT. GREEN ~ LT. BLUE)

STAR STRIPS

ANGEL CARD

Materials needed: construction paper, glue, scissors

Fold 9-inch by 12-inch pink paper twice (Fig. 2). Fold 3-inch by 6-inch white paper (Fig. 3), and cut out angels. Cut out panels for gowns and white strips for star. Glue together as shown.

THREE KINGS CARD

Materials needed: construction paper, glue, gold lace paper doily, gold foil paper, scissors

Fold a 9-inch by 12-inch sheet of white paper in the middle (Fig. 1). Then fold in three equal sections (Fig. 2). Place pattern on folded paper and cut out kings (Fig. 3). Fold down A's and glue (Fig. 4). Cut out two purple and one green of the panels and ornaments and glue on fronts of kings (green on center king). Cut out and glue faces. Cut out three sections of doily and glue over panels. Cut gifts from gold paper and glue in position. The kings will stand.

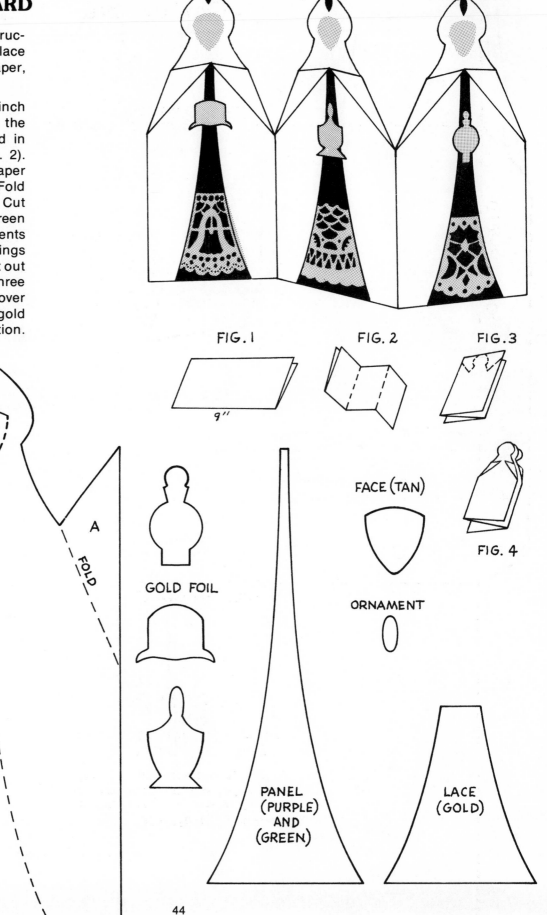

FIG. 1

9"

FIG. 2

FIG. 3

FIG. 4

GOLD FOIL

FACE (TAN)

ORNAMENT

A

A

FOLD

FOLD

(WHITE)

PANEL
(PURPLE)
AND
(GREEN)

LACE
(GOLD)

44

4½" X 6" ENVELOPE

FOLD FORWARD

FOLD FORWARD

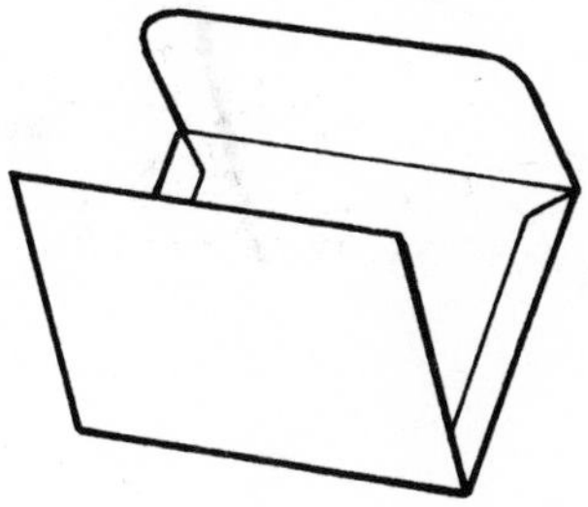

FOLD FORWARD

GLUE **B**

GLUE A

FOLD FORWARD

B

A

ENVELOPE

Materials needed: construction paper, glue, scissors

To make a 4½-inch by 6-inch envelope, cut out and fold as shown. Glue A to A and B to B. Fold top flap down last.

45

FLAP I

Christmas Ornaments and Decorations

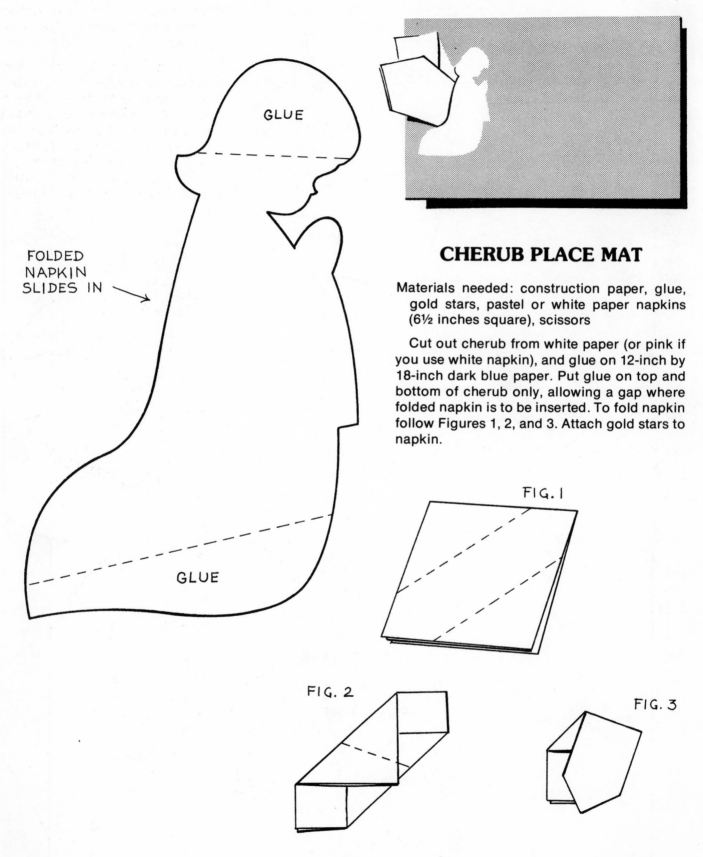

GLUE

FOLDED
NAPKIN
SLIDES IN

GLUE

CHERUB PLACE MAT

Materials needed: construction paper, glue, gold stars, pastel or white paper napkins (6½ inches square), scissors

Cut out cherub from white paper (or pink if you use white napkin), and glue on 12-inch by 18-inch dark blue paper. Put glue on top and bottom of cherub only, allowing a gap where folded napkin is to be inserted. To fold napkin follow Figures 1, 2, and 3. Attach gold stars to napkin.

FIG. 1

FIG. 2

FIG. 3

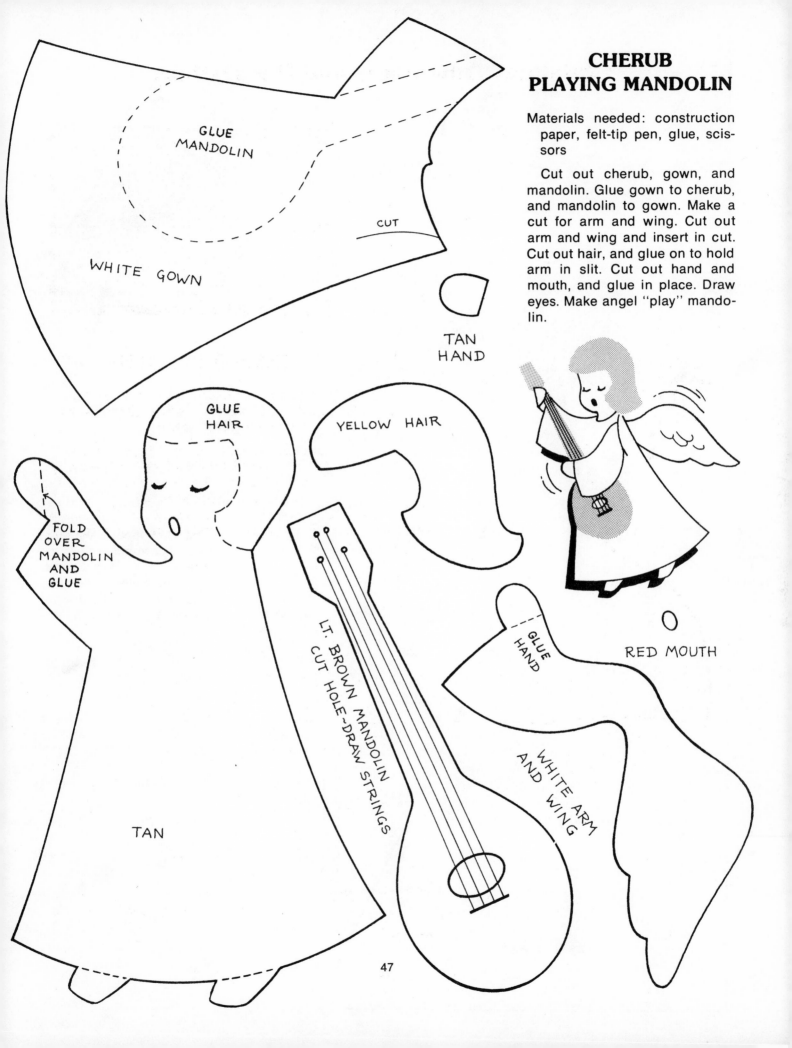

GLUE MANDOLIN

WHITE GOWN

CUT

CHERUB PLAYING MANDOLIN

Materials needed: construction paper, felt-tip pen, glue, scissors

Cut out cherub, gown, and mandolin. Glue gown to cherub, and mandolin to gown. Make a cut for arm and wing. Cut out arm and wing and insert in cut. Cut out hair, and glue on to hold arm in slit. Cut out hand and mouth, and glue in place. Draw eyes. Make angel "play" mandolin.

TAN HAND

GLUE HAIR

YELLOW HAIR

FOLD OVER MANDOLIN AND GLUE

LT. BROWN MANDOLIN CUT HOLE-DRAW STRINGS

GLUE HAND

RED MOUTH

TAN

WHITE ARM AND WING

47

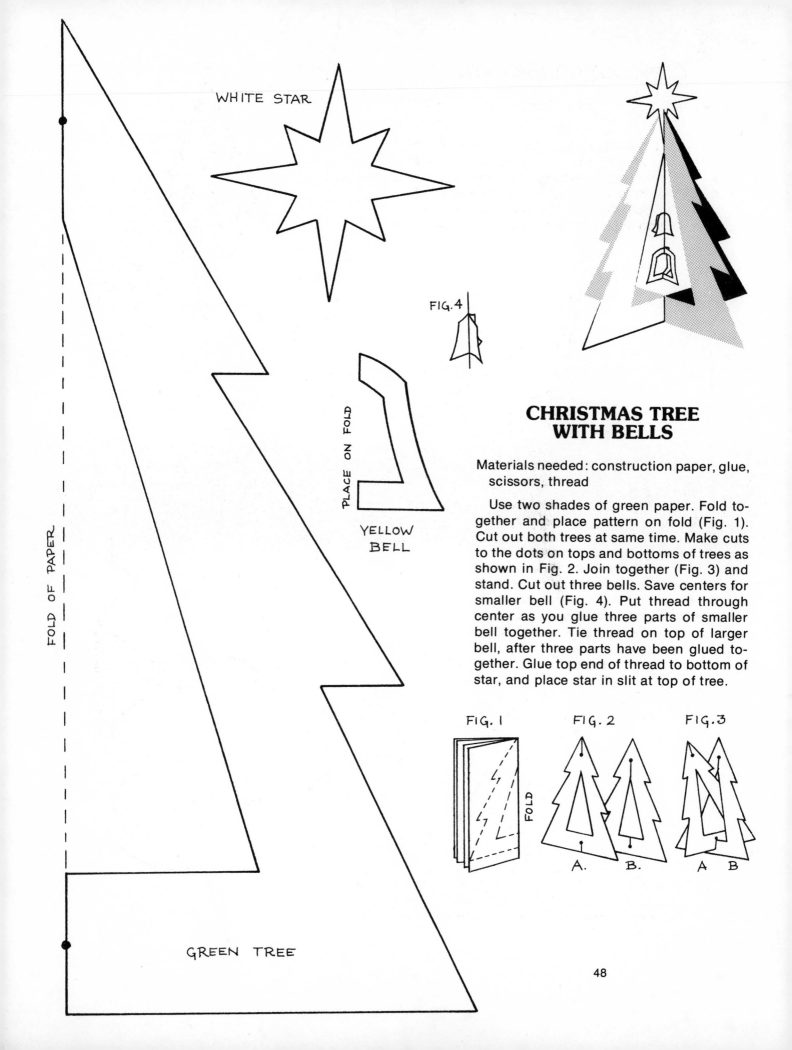

WHITE STAR

FIG.4

PLACE ON FOLD

YELLOW BELL

FOLD OF PAPER

GREEN TREE

CHRISTMAS TREE WITH BELLS

Materials needed: construction paper, glue, scissors, thread

Use two shades of green paper. Fold together and place pattern on fold (Fig. 1). Cut out both trees at same time. Make cuts to the dots on tops and bottoms of trees as shown in Fig. 2. Join together (Fig. 3) and stand. Cut out three bells. Save centers for smaller bell (Fig. 4). Put thread through center as you glue three parts of smaller bell together. Tie thread on top of larger bell, after three parts have been glued together. Glue top end of thread to bottom of star, and place star in slit at top of tree.

FIG. I

FOLD

FIG. 2

A.   B.

FIG.3

A   B

48

HANGING ORNAMENTS

Materials needed: construction paper, glue, scissors, thread

Each ornament has three sides and can be made of one color or three different colors (such as red, green, and white). Place patterns on folds of paper, and cut. Cut designs while paper is still folded. (It would be fun to make your own designs.) Fold and glue, matching flaps together. Hang with thread.

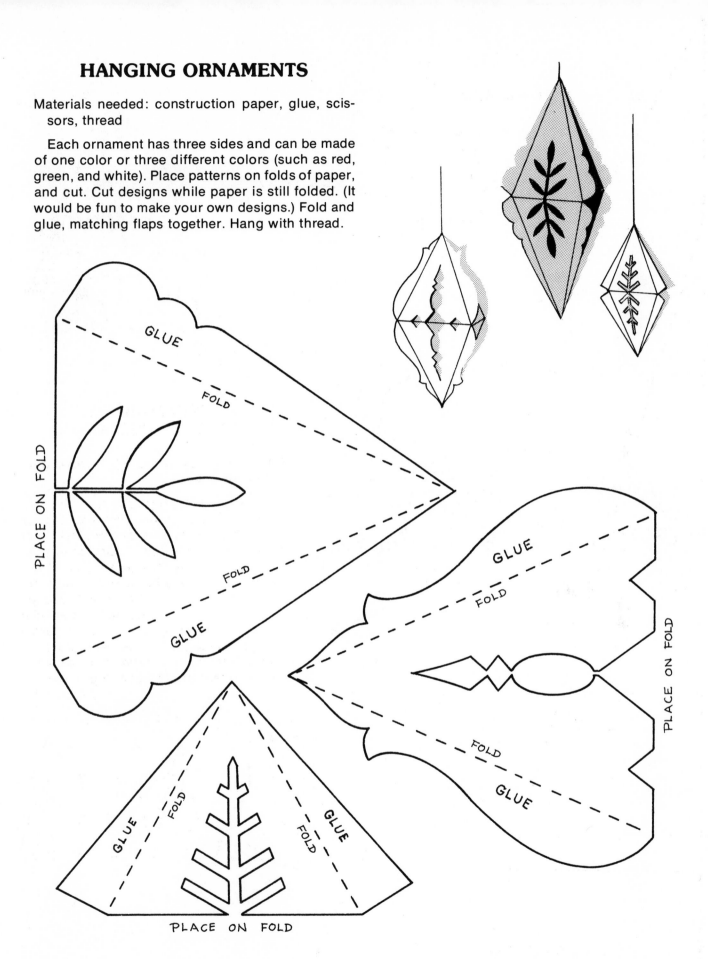

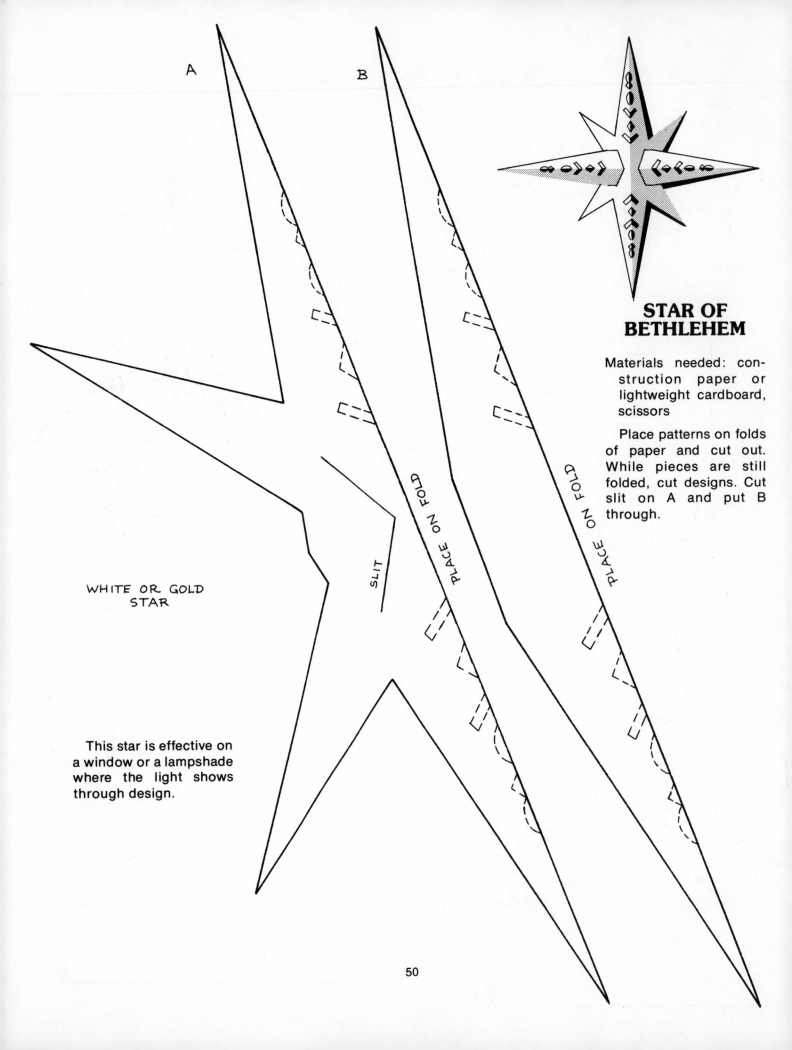

A

B

STAR OF BETHLEHEM

Materials needed: construction paper or lightweight cardboard, scissors

Place patterns on folds of paper and cut out. While pieces are still folded, cut designs. Cut slit on A and put B through.

SLIT

PLACE ON FOLD

PLACE ON FOLD

WHITE OR GOLD
STAR

This star is effective on a window or a lampshade where the light shows through design.

Christmas Story Scenes

MANGER SCENE

Materials needed: construction paper, glue, scissors

Cut out two figures of Joseph, and glue together from the waist up. (Leave the lower half free to be spread open, allowing the figure to stand.) Cut out head, hair, hands, robe, and staff, and glue in place.

Cut out two figures of Mary, and glue top half together. Cut out veil, and glue in place. Cut out hands and face, and glue to figure.

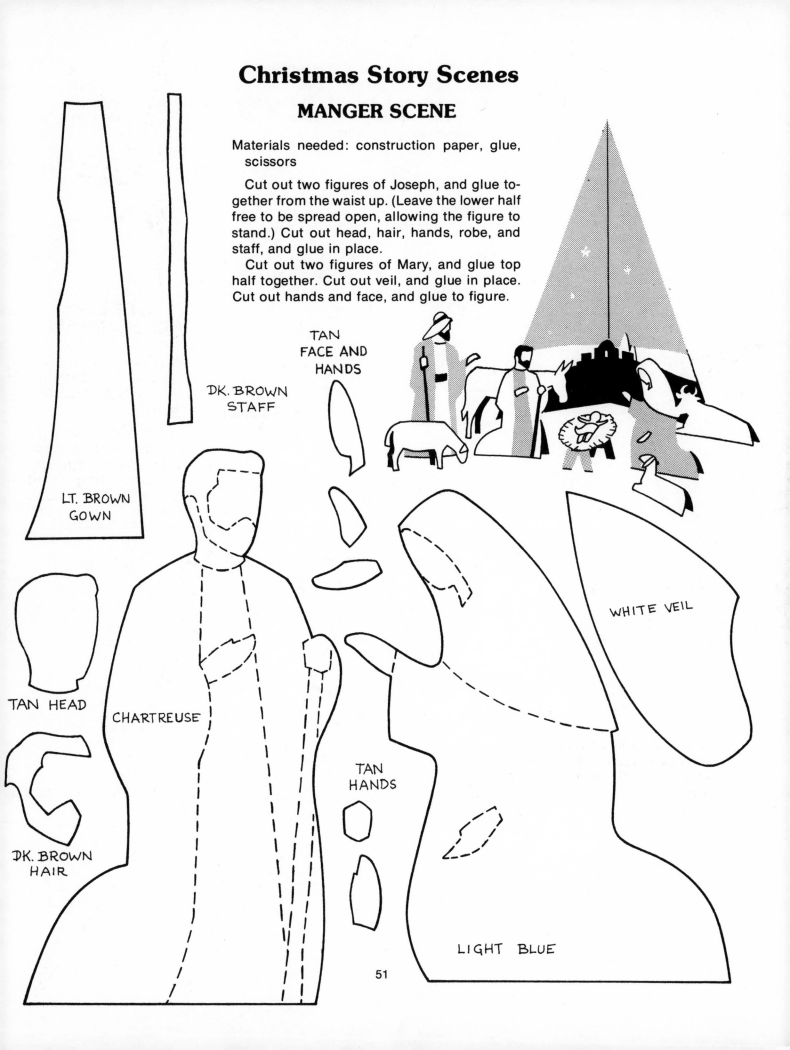

LT. BROWN GOWN

DK. BROWN STAFF

TAN FACE AND HANDS

TAN HEAD

CHARTREUSE

DK. BROWN HAIR

TAN HANDS

WHITE VEIL

LIGHT BLUE

Cut out manger, and fit together (Fig. 1). Cut out straw, and glue to manger. Cut out infant and cloth, and glue to straw. Place donkey and sheep patterns on folds of paper, and cut out. Insert ears on donkey before gluing heads together. Glue heads of sheep before putting on the ears.

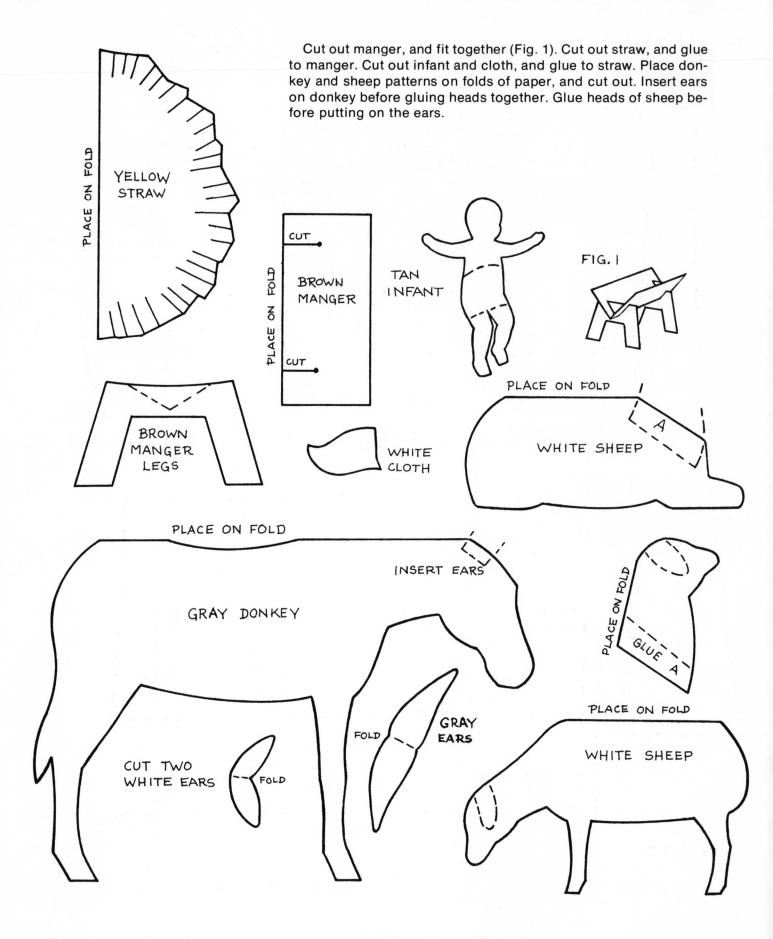

PLACE ON FOLD

YELLOW STRAW

CUT

BROWN MANGER

PLACE ON FOLD

CUT

TAN INFANT

FIG. 1

BROWN MANGER LEGS

WHITE CLOTH

PLACE ON FOLD

WHITE SHEEP

A

PLACE ON FOLD

INSERT EARS

GRAY DONKEY

PLACE ON FOLD

GLUE A

CUT TWO WHITE EARS

FOLD

FOLD

GRAY EARS

PLACE ON FOLD

WHITE SHEEP

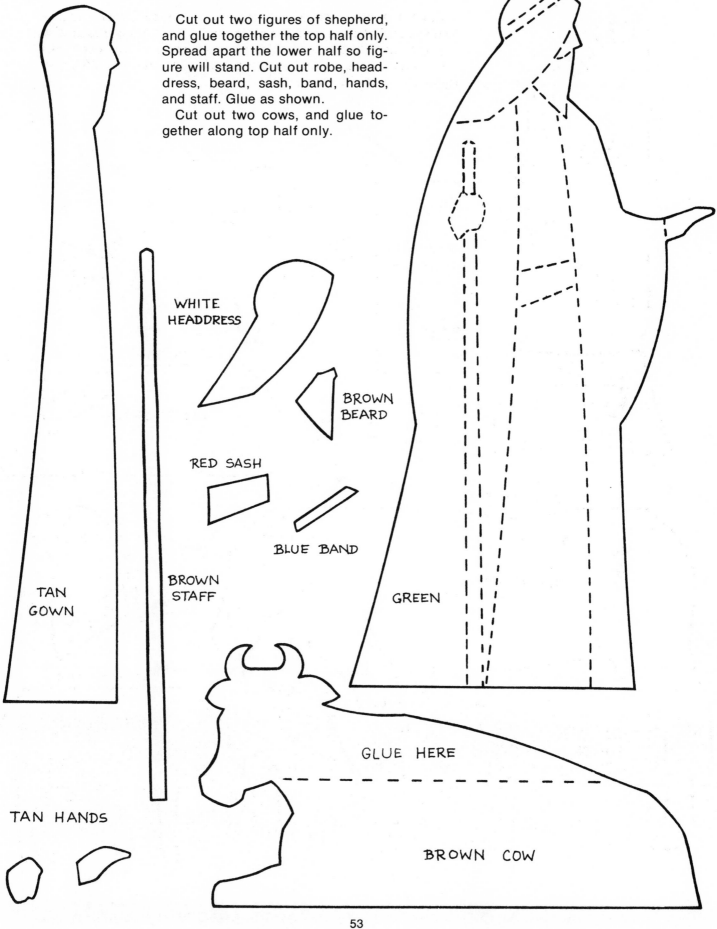

Cut out two figures of shepherd, and glue together the top half only. Spread apart the lower half so figure will stand. Cut out robe, headdress, beard, sash, band, hands, and staff. Glue as shown.

Cut out two cows, and glue together along top half only.

WHITE HEADDRESS

BROWN BEARD

RED SASH

BLUE BAND

TAN GOWN

BROWN STAFF

GREEN

GLUE HERE

TAN HANDS

BROWN COW

Fold construction paper in half, and place patterns against folds as indicated. Cut out sky, hills, and scene. Open and glue hills and scene onto sky. Reverse the fold so it will stand (Fig. 1) to form a backdrop for figures of manger scene. Glue four small, white stars onto sky.

STARS

GLUE STAR

PURPLE SCENE

PLACE ON FOLD

PLACE ON FOLD

GREEN TREES

BLUE SKY

LAVENDER HILLS

FIG. 1

PLACE ON FOLD

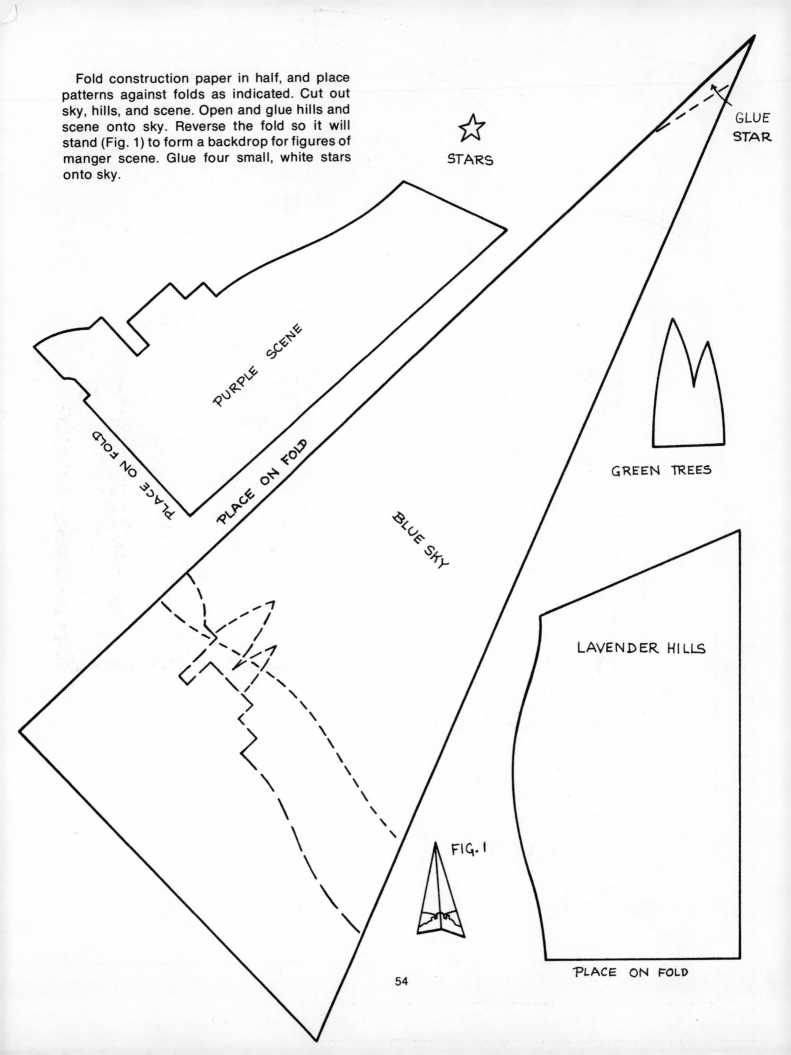

THREE KINGS WINDOW

Materials needed: construction paper, glue, scissors

Place window frame pattern against the fold of black paper, and cut out. Glue frame to dark blue paper (9 inches by 11 inches).

To make king No. 1, start by cutting out entire figure from purple paper. Then cut out and glue on panel, hands, chalice, face, and crown. Glue in position on the dark blue paper.

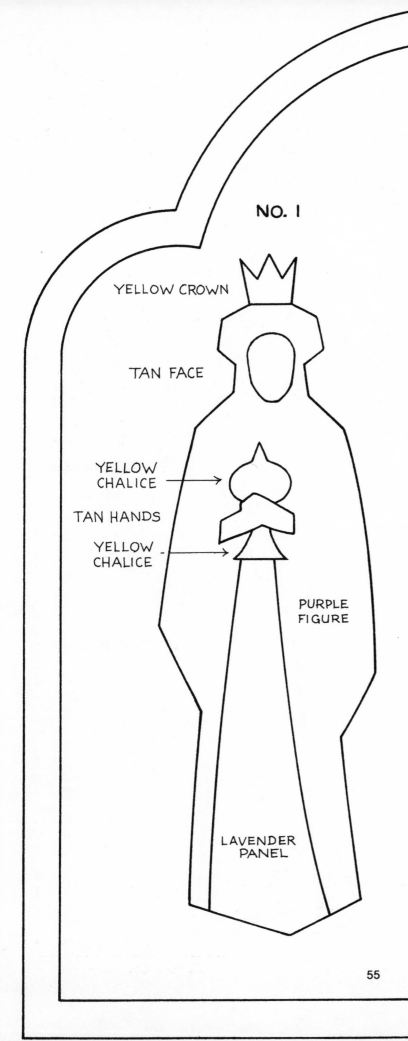

NO. I

YELLOW CROWN

TAN FACE

YELLOW CHALICE

TAN HANDS

YELLOW CHALICE

PURPLE FIGURE

LAVENDER PANEL

55

← PLACE ON FOLD

For king No. 2, start by cutting out white headdress and robe. Cut out face, hands, ornament, and box. Glue these in position. Then cut out and add red panel.

For king No. 3, start by cutting out green robe. Cut out sleeves, hands, vase, and dark green panel, and glue in position. Next, cut out face, beard, and crown, and glue on king. Position king on the background as shown, and then add white stars.

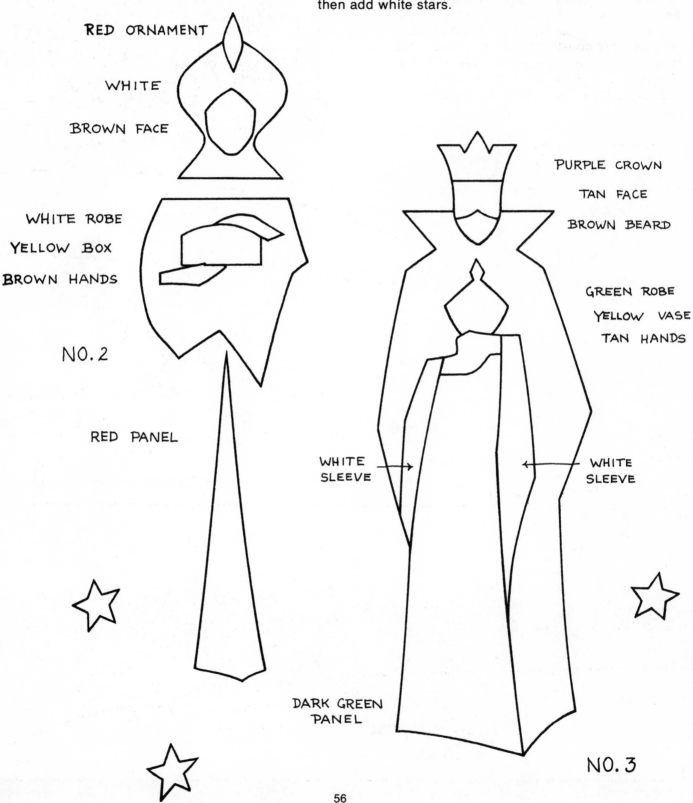

RED ORNAMENT

WHITE

BROWN FACE

WHITE ROBE
YELLOW BOX
BROWN HANDS

NO. 2

RED PANEL

PURPLE CROWN

TAN FACE

BROWN BEARD

GREEN ROBE
YELLOW VASE
TAN HANDS

WHITE
SLEEVE

WHITE
SLEEVE

DARK GREEN
PANEL

NO. 3

THE CHRISTMAS STORY

Materials needed: construction paper, 9-inch by 12-inch box lid, glue, scissors

Make a stage by gluing dark blue paper against inside back of box lid. Cut out lavender hills and purple buildings, and glue across the bottom of blue lining of box. Cut out a star and glue in sky. Cut out the different scenes from colors of construction paper noted. Glue as shown. Cut slits in top and sides of lid, for scenes to be slipped through as the story is told. Cut out valance, and glue across top of lid.

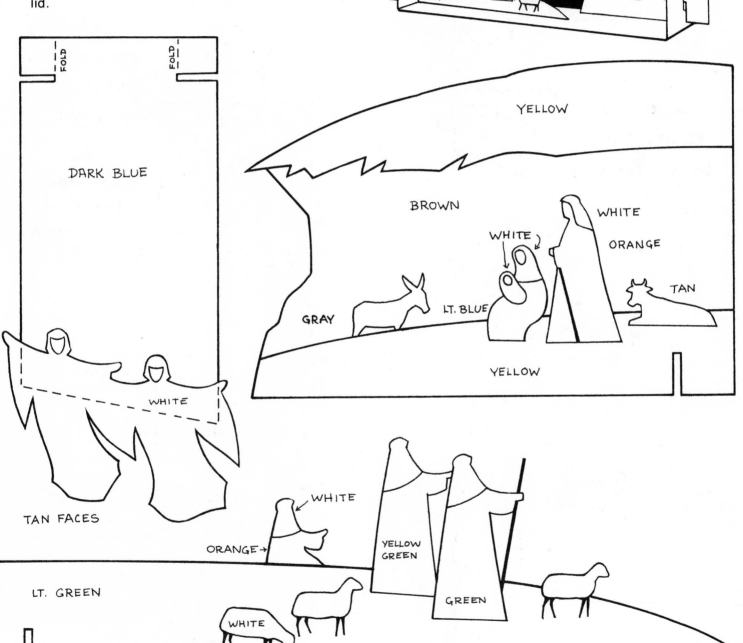

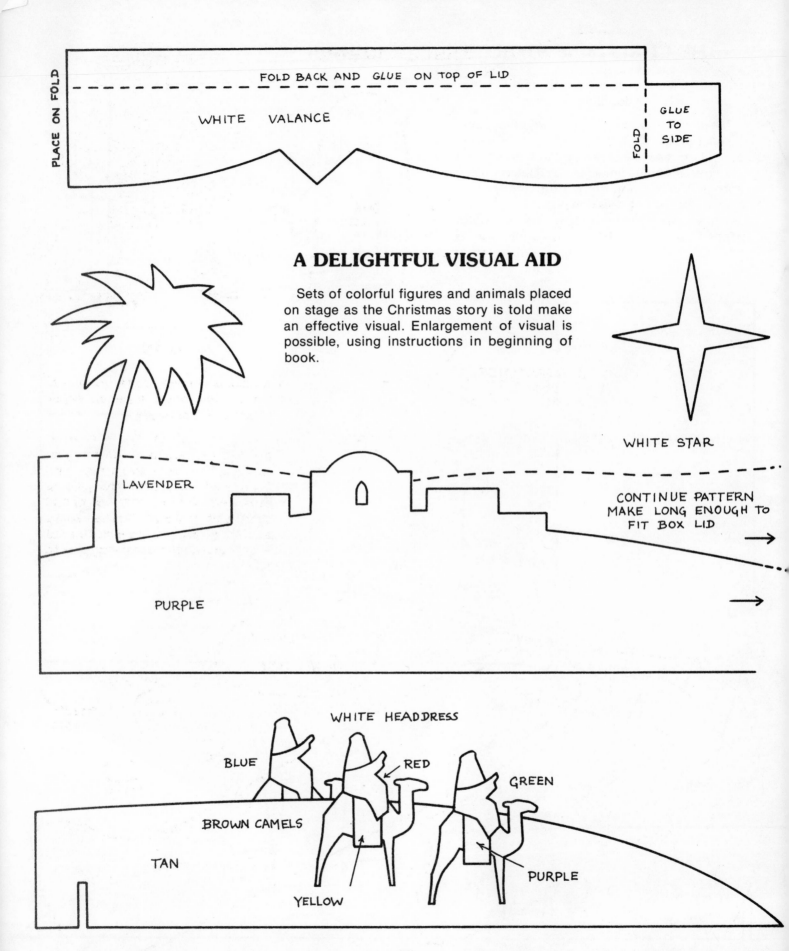

PLACE ON FOLD

FOLD BACK AND GLUE ON TOP OF LID

WHITE VALANCE

FOLD

GLUE TO SIDE

A DELIGHTFUL VISUAL AID

Sets of colorful figures and animals placed on stage as the Christmas story is told make an effective visual. Enlargement of visual is possible, using instructions in beginning of book.

WHITE STAR

LAVENDER

PURPLE

CONTINUE PATTERN MAKE LONG ENOUGH TO FIT BOX LID

WHITE HEADDRESS

BLUE

RED

GREEN

BROWN CAMELS

TAN

PURPLE

YELLOW

58

Miscellaneous

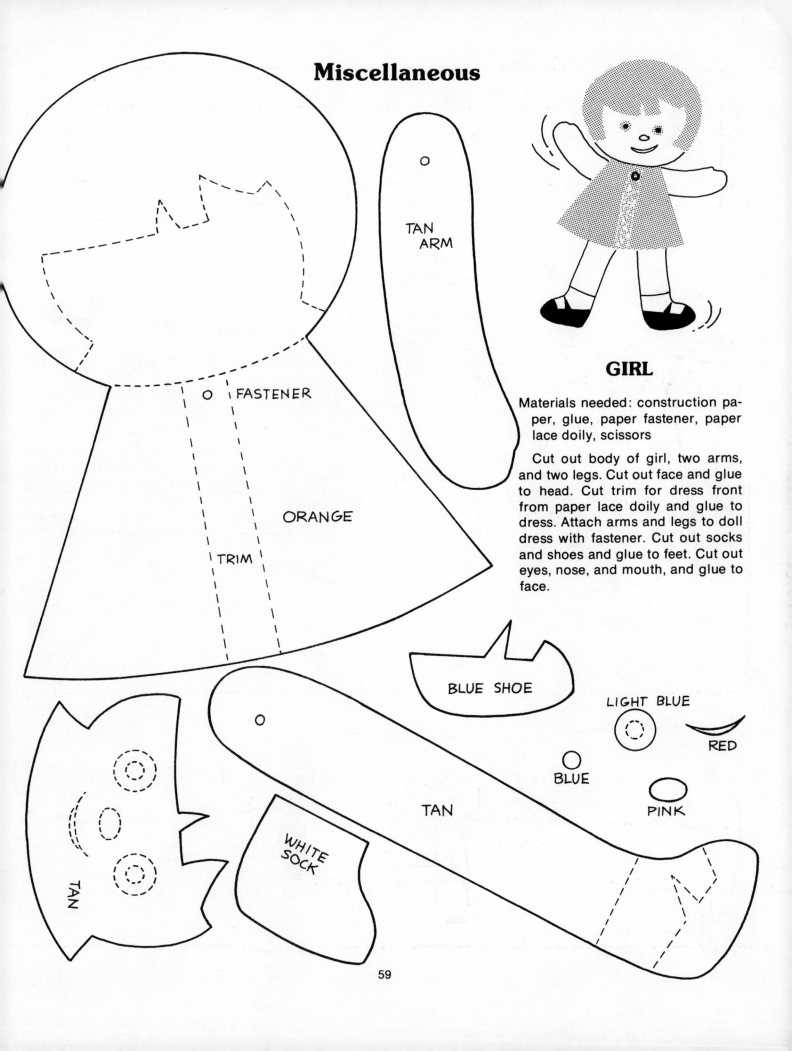

TAN ARM

O FASTENER

ORANGE

TRIM

GIRL

Materials needed: construction paper, glue, paper fastener, paper lace doily, scissors

Cut out body of girl, two arms, and two legs. Cut out face and glue to head. Cut trim for dress front from paper lace doily and glue to dress. Attach arms and legs to doll dress with fastener. Cut out socks and shoes and glue to feet. Cut out eyes, nose, and mouth, and glue to face.

BLUE SHOE

LIGHT BLUE

RED

BLUE

PINK

TAN

TAN

WHITE SOCK

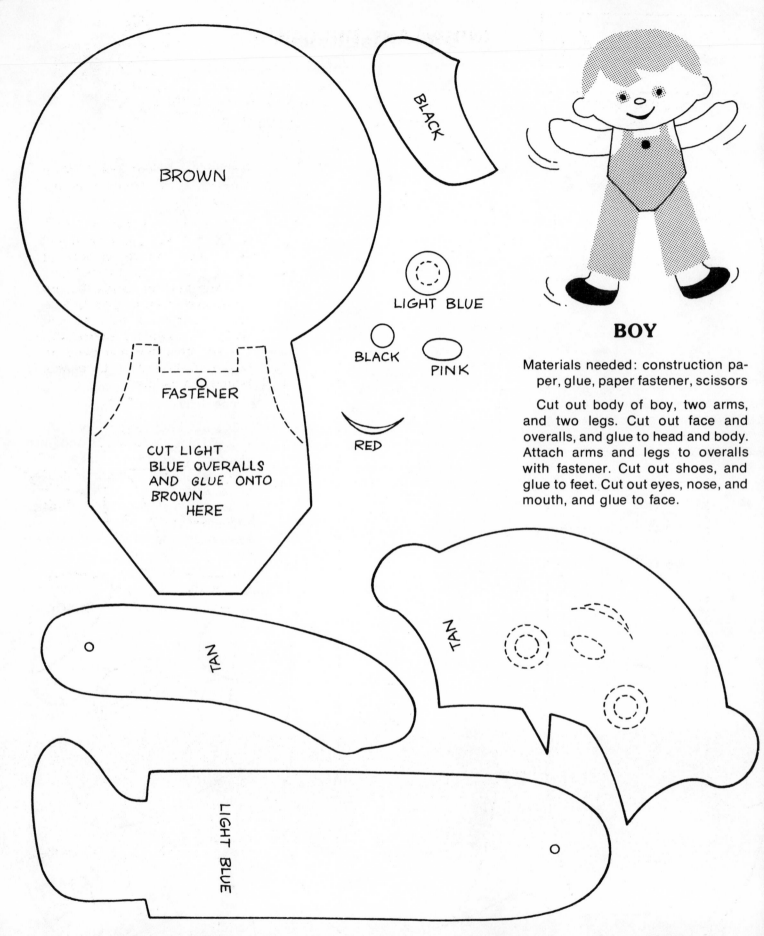

BROWN

BLACK

LIGHT BLUE

BLACK

PINK

RED

FASTENER

CUT LIGHT
BLUE OVERALLS
AND GLUE ONTO
BROWN
HERE

TAN

TAN

LIGHT BLUE

BOY

Materials needed: construction paper, glue, paper fastener, scissors

Cut out body of boy, two arms, and two legs. Cut out face and overalls, and glue to head and body. Attach arms and legs to overalls with fastener. Cut out shoes, and glue to feet. Cut out eyes, nose, and mouth, and glue to face.

INDIAN AND HIS CANOE

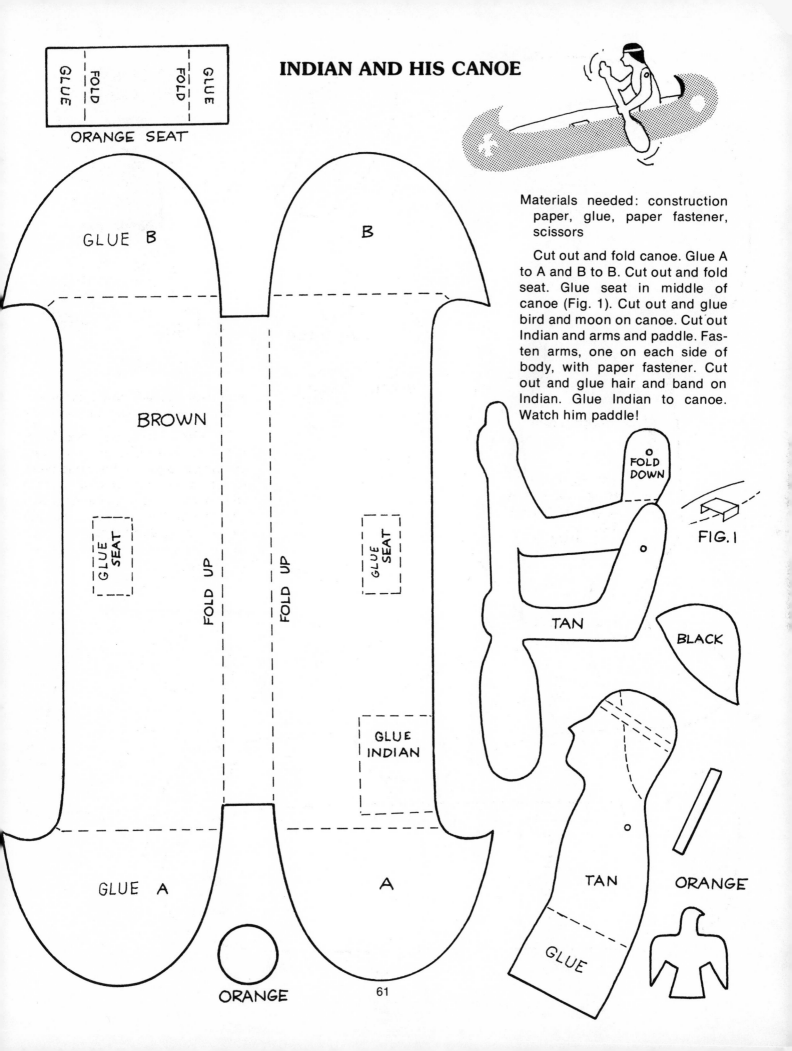

ORANGE SEAT

GLUE

FOLD

GLUE

FOLD

GLUE

GLUE B

B

BROWN

GLUE SEAT

GLUE SEAT

FOLD UP

FOLD UP

GLUE INDIAN

GLUE A

A

ORANGE

Materials needed: construction paper, glue, paper fastener, scissors

Cut out and fold canoe. Glue A to A and B to B. Cut out and fold seat. Glue seat in middle of canoe (Fig. 1). Cut out and glue bird and moon on canoe. Cut out Indian and arms and paddle. Fasten arms, one on each side of body, with paper fastener. Cut out and glue hair and band on Indian. Glue Indian to canoe. Watch him paddle!

FOLD DOWN

FIG. 1

TAN

BLACK

TAN

ORANGE

GLUE

61

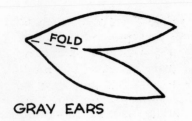

GRAY EARS

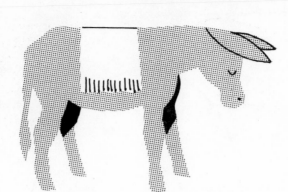

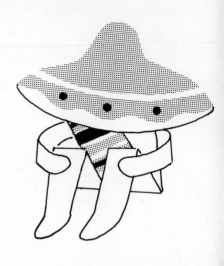

○

RED DOTS

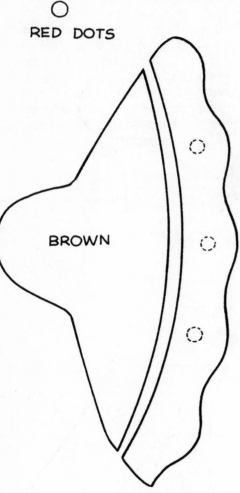

BROWN

MEXICAN AND BURRO

Materials needed: construction paper, felt-tip pen, glue, scissors

Place burro pattern on fold of paper and cut out. Glue together top half only. Cut out ears, and glue to head. Place blanket pattern on fold, and cut out. Fringe the edge, and glue blanket to burro's back.

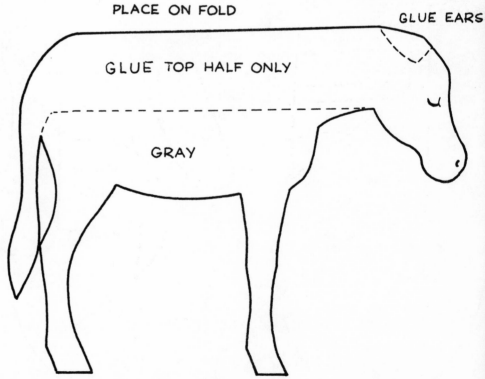

PLACE ON FOLD

GLUE EARS

GLUE TOP HALF ONLY

GRAY

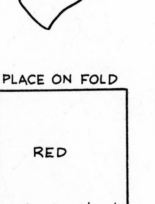

PLACE ON FOLD

RED

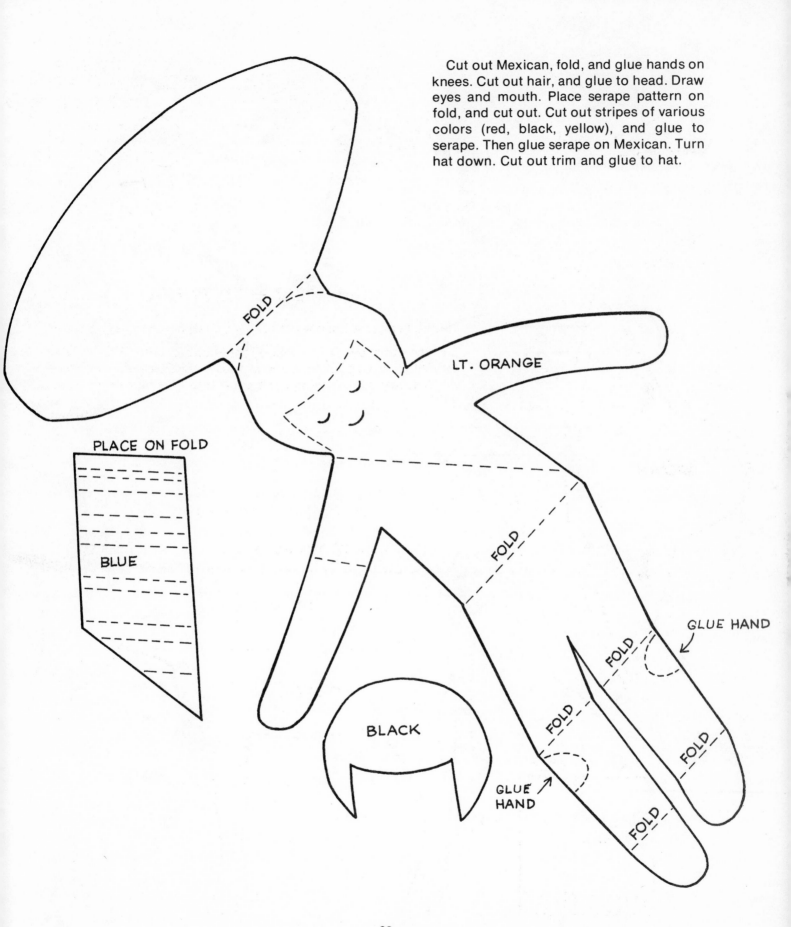

Cut out Mexican, fold, and glue hands on knees. Cut out hair, and glue to head. Draw eyes and mouth. Place serape pattern on fold, and cut out. Cut out stripes of various colors (red, black, yellow), and glue to serape. Then glue serape on Mexican. Turn hat down. Cut out trim and glue to hat.

FOLD

LT. ORANGE

PLACE ON FOLD

BLUE

FOLD

GLUE HAND

FOLD

FOLD

FOLD

FOLD

FOLD

BLACK

GLUE HAND

CLOCK

Materials needed: construction paper, 9-inch paper
plate, paper fastener, scissors, string

Punch a hole in center of paper plate. Cut out hands.
Insert fastener in hole in hands, then through plate.
Draw on numbers and border design, and hang with
string.

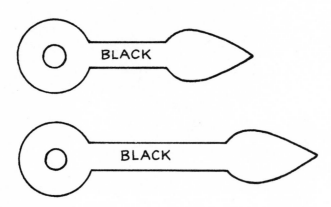